TORAH TOONS I

THE BOOK

CREATED BY JOEL LURIE GRISHAVER
TORAH AURA PRODUCTIONS

THIS BOOK IS DEDICATED TO EARL AUERBACH
JANE AND ALAN
AND TO DAYS OF KRISHNA CAT

First Edition

STUDENT INTRODUCTION

When I was a kid, I spent a lot of time doodling on the back of dittoed handouts they always want you to take home from school, and the margins of old homework assignments. I did it often, because I just wanted to figure out how something might look, or because I wanted to create my version of something I read. Since then, I've done a reasonable job of growing up and the doodling has turned into a way of earning a living - drawing cartoons to go with the curriculum materials I write. A few years ago, I was working for the Los Angeles Hebrew High School, and I began doing a thing called TORAH-TOONS. I'd draw these huge poster sized drawings of the weekly TORAH PORTION, and hang them on clothes-lines during the service. When we started TORAH AURA PRODUCTIONS, TORAH TOONS became a media series. Now, TORAH-TOONS is a book. Just like the first doodles I used to do in class, TORAH-TOONS is my way of figuring out how things in the TORAH might look, and a way of working out my own version of what the portions mean. Have the same fun with it - we did in producing it, draw your own doodles and figure out your own versions.

CHAZAK, CHAZAK V'NIT-CHAZEIK: The Gris.

TEACHER'S INTRODUCTION

Parshat Ha Shavua (studying the weekly Torah Portion) is an important Jewish process. It does many things. It takes the Jew on a annual journey through the entire Torah. It creates a background through which all kinds of major Jewish issues, themes and ideas are considered and reconsidered. And, perhaps most importantly, weekly study of the parsha creates a special sense of community - allowing participants to share their own insights and reactions. TORAH-TOONS is a curriculum package which tries to create the process of parshat ha-shavua for students who don't live in the mileau of the TORAH.

TORAH-TOONS I is a set of 36 slide-tape segments designed to provide a single lesson on each of the first 36 parshiot of the TORAH (a standard school year). This TORAH-TOONS book contains worksheets and exercises to go with each of these segments. They include a portion of the biblical text (which is the focus), a selection of rabbinic commentary, and some kind of open-ended exercise. In going through this material, you will (1) learn something about the process of Jewish Torah Study, (2) come to understand the style of serval of the major commentators, and (3) cover a large number of related Jewish topics.

This book, while it can be used independant text, has been designed to used in conjunction with TORAH-TOONS media. There is a detailed teacher's guide, and a set of TORAH-TOONS GAMING PACS. In addition, there is a program called THE MAZE, THE THORN FOREST, THE BOILING POT AND THE WELL - which services as an introduction to the process of biblical commentary. Using these resources may enhance your teaching process.

Enjoy TORAH-TOONS and have fun teaching with it.

JANE GOLUB   JOEL LURIE GRISHAVER   ALAN ROWE

Special thanks to Dr. Stuart Kelman

It is Jewish to study
the Torah once a week.
The Torah has been broken
into parshiot and by studying
all these 'Torah Portions'
you can go through the entire
Torah in a year of studying
weekly parshiot.

It is Jewish to do Torah
study by getting together with
a good friend of a small group
Torah study is a combination of
reading, discussing, guessing,
remembering and finding your own
understandings. Torah study is a
combination of uncovering answers
that other people who've studied
the Torah have found, and finding
your own meaning in the text.
Torah study is a way of making
friends, forming community and
doing Jewish learning.

The Torah is like a library. It is made up of all kinds of Jewish
literature. It is filled with stories, poems, pieces of history,
collections of laws and other kinds of writings. It has everything
from farming tips to blueprints for buildings. When we go through
the Torah, we can learn about the history of the Jewish people, the
stories which have been important to our people, Jewish laws and
customs, and almost every important Jewish idea and value. Going
through the Torah takes us on a guided tour of almost everything
Jewish, because most Jewish things either have their origin in the
Torah, or because something in the Torah will remind us of them anyway.

The Torah has been studied by Jews
in every age and in every Jewish
community. Jews all over the world
are exploring the same sidre during
the same week.

When we study Torah, we not only
look at our own opinions, but match
them with the questions and answers
of the generations who have gone
through the text before us.

The study of parshat ha shavua
doesn't only teach us something
about the Torah. It also introduces us to other Jews in different
places and times, who have also
looked for meaning in the same words.

The rabbis were a group of Jewish scholars who lived in Eretz Yisrael and in Babylon between 200 B.C.E. and 500 C.E. They were the ones who wrote the Talmud, the Siddur, the Haggada for Pesach and much of what is important to us as basic Jewish sources. One of the ways they studied the Torah was through a kind of way of learning called midrash. Midrash was a way of reading the Torah and fitting pieces together from all over the text - sort of weaving one story into another. Midrash was a way of writing down new stories between the lines of the stories found in the Torah. These stories still kept all the facts of the original Torah stories, but gave new answers and understandings. And, Midrash was a way of inventing new stories, parables about Kings and princes, stories which by comparison help us to understand the points the Torah is making.

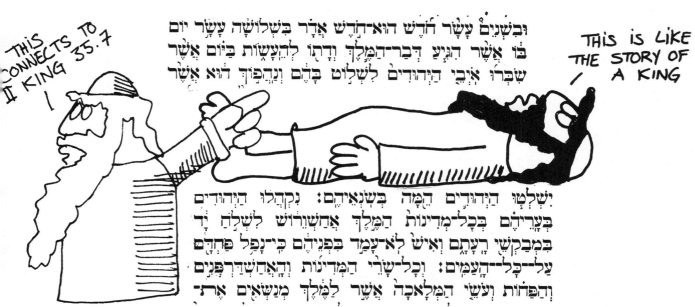

This book is based on midrash. Every week, you will find a piece of Torah with some questions. First you'll work out your own answers to these questions, and then you'll see how the midrash answered them. You'll learn - not only about the Torah - but about a whole new way of thinking called midrash.

TABLE OF CONTENTS

In parashat BERESHIT God creates the world. This is done in
seven days. On the first day, light is created. On the second
day, there is a division of the waters. On the third day, dry
land appears and plants begin to grow. On the fourth day, God
creates the things which give light - the sun, moon and stars.
On the fifth day, birds and fish are created. And, on the sixth
day, God creates animals and people. On the seventh day God
rested.

Next, the sidra tells the story of what happens in the Garden of
Eden. The garden is described, and Adam then Hava are created.

The garden has a tree in the center - the tree of life, and the
tree of the knowledge of good and evil. Adam and Hava are told
not to eat from the tree, but do so under the urging of the
snake. God then sends Adam and Hava from the garden.

Once outside the garden, Adam and Hava have two sons: Cain and
Havel. Cain is a farmer and Havel is a shepherd. Both offer
sacrifices to God, but God accepts only Havel's offering. The
two then fight and Cain kills Havel. God then marks Cain.

The sidra ends with a list of the ten generations from Adam to
Noach.

Here is the way the Torah tells the story of Cain and Havel. As you read it, see if you can figure out (1) Why God rejected Cain's offering, and (2) Why God didn't stop the fight between the brothers?

And Adam had relations with Hava his wife
and she became pregnant and gave birth to Cain
And she said: "I have gotten a man with the help of the Lord."
And again she gave birth - to his brother Havel.
Havel was a keeper of sheep - but Cain was a tiller of the
    ground.
After a while it came to pass
that Cain brought the fruit of the ground as an offering to the
Lord.
Havel also brought the first born of his flock.
And the Lord accepted Havel and his offering -
But did not accept Cain and his offering.
And Cain was very upset - he was depressed.
And the Lord said to Cain:"Why are you angry and why are you
depressed? If you do well - won't it be lifted high?
And if you do not do well - sin is before the entrance -
    like one who crouches with desires towards you -
    but you can rule over him."
And Cain spoke to his brother Havel
And it came to pass when they were in the field
That Cain rose up against his brother Havel and killed him.

And the Lord said to Cain: "Where is Havel your brother?"
And he said: "I don't know. Am I my brother's keeper?"
And He said: "What have you done? The voice of your brother's
    blood cries out to me from the ground." Gen. 4:1-10

1. Why do you think God accepted Havel's offering and not Cain's.?

_____

_____

_____

2. Why do you think God started the fight between Cain and Havel and then didn't stop it?

_____

_____

_____

A MIDRASH (Gen. R. 22.8ff)

The slaying of Havel by Cain wasn't a total surprise. The two
brothers often fought. This is why Adam, their father, gave
them different jobs. He made Cain a farmer and Havel a
shepherd. This fight however started with their sacrifices.
Adam told his sons that they had to offer the first of their new
crops and herds to God. Havel selected the best of his flocks,
but Cain offered that which was left over after his own meal.
That is why God rejected Cain's offering.

Cain blamed his brother and told him: "Let's separate and divide
our possessions."
He told Havel: "Take the sheep and cattle and I will take the
land." Havel agreed. The next day Cain told Havel: "Get
yourself and your herd off of my land - I own the earth." Havel
answered: "Your clothing is made out of wool - take it off - I
own it." This is the way the fight began.

**A. Underline the parts of this midrash which are not told to us
in the Torah.**

B. What facts from the Torah does this midrash use?

_____
_____
_____

**C. According to this midrash, what is the reason that God
rejected Cain's offering?**

_____
_____
_____

D. What message does this midrash teach?

_____
_____

A MIDRASH (Ibid)

You might think that God in this story was like a king watching
two gladiators fighting. If one of the gladiators is killed -
it would be the king's fault because he didn't stop the contest.
Cain asked God: "Isn't it Your fault, because You did not
command me to stop?" God answered: "I made you in My image
with a brain and a soul. Were I to direct your every action you
would be just like a puppet. You have a will of your own and
you are responsible for your actions."

**A. Underline the parts of this midrash which can be found in
the Torah. (Hint: it may not come from this story).**

B. According to the midrash - Why didn't God stop Cain?
_____
_____

C. What moral is taught by this midrash?
_____
_____
_____

In parshat NOACH we find that world has been filled with violence. God decides to flood the world and save only one family. God turns to Noach, the one righteous man and orders him to build an ark to save himself, his family and animal life from the flood which will soon follow. Noach follows instructions.

The group spends 7 days in the ark before the rain.
It then rains for 40 days and 40 nights.
For 150 days the water rises.
For 150 days the water then goes down - enough for the mountain tops to be seen.
Then Noah waits 40 more days and sends out a raven to look for
     dryland.
7 days later Noach sends a dove to look for dry land and it returns with an olive branch.
And 7 days later the dove flies off for good.

Noach and company leave the ark. They offer sacrifices to God and a rainbow appears as the sign of a covenant that God will never again destroy the earth. Noach also ferments the first grapes and gets drunk.

A group of people gather in the Shinar valley and try to build a tower up to the heavens. God stops them by making them speak many different languages. The place is called Bavel.

At the end of the sidra, we are given the 10 generations from Noach to Avram, and a quick preview of the Avram's story.

Here is the way the Torah tells the story of the Tower of Bavel.
As you read it, see if you can figure out why God wanted to stop
people from building a tower.

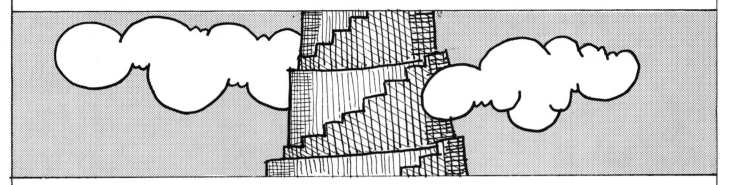

All over the earth was the same language and the same words.
And as people wandered to the east - they found a valley in the
land of Shinar and settled there.
They said to each other: "Come-now let us make bricks and bake
them hard."
So they had brick-stone rather than building stone and the raw
asphalt could be used instead of red-mortar.
Now they said: "Come-now, let us build a city and a tower with
its top reaching heaven,
and let us make a name for ourselves - otherwise we'll be
scattered all over the face of the earth."

The LORD came down to see the city and the tower which the
people had built.
The LORD said: "Here is one people, with one language for all of
them,
And this is the start of their actions,
From now on, nothing they plan to do will be out of their reach.
Come-now let us go down and confuse their speech - so that no
one will understand what another has said."
Thus the Lord scattered them from there over the face of all the
earth so they had to stop building the city
This is why it is called Bavel - because the LORD confused the
speech of the whole earth.

Gen. 11:1-9

**Why was God angry that the people were building a tower and a
city?**

_____

_____

_____

**Do you think that God was really afraid of what the people were
doing?**

_____

_____

_____

_____

A MIDRASH (Pirke D'Rabbi Eliezer 24)

The tower was built with careful planning. On the east side were steps which were used to go up and on the westside was a down staircase. The tower got to be so high that it took a year to reach the top. People cared more about the bricks than they did about other people. If a person fell - no one cried. But if a brick were dropped, the workmen cried and tore out their hair - because it would take a year to replace it.

People lived all their lives on the tower. They married, had children and raised them without setting foot on the ground. Nimrod, the leader of the group cared only about finishing the tower. Often he would send up bricks but no food. Only when the workers refused to continue would the food be sent.

A. What facts from the Torah does this midrash use?

_____
_____
_____

B. What reasons does this midrash give for God being angry at the way the tower was being built?

_____
_____
_____

C. What is the message of this midrash?

_____
_____
_____

LECH LECHA is the sidra which begins the stories of
Avram/Avraham. In this parasha, Avram is called by God and
moves to the land of Canaan. He moves there with his wife
Sarai/Sara, and with Lot, his brother's son.

Shortly after their arrival in Canaan, a famine breaks out and
the family moves to Egypt. There, Pharaoh falls in love with
Sarai, and Avram tells him "She is my sister." When Pharaoh
finds out the truth, he gives Avram a great deal of wealth.
(This is the first "WIFE-SISTER" story). The family then
returns to Canaan.

There, Avram and Lot split up, with Lot moving near the city of
Sodom. Next, the war of the kings breaks out; and Lot is taken
as a hostage. Avram enters the campaign, and rescues Lot.
Melkitzedek, a local king praises Avram and his God.

God and Avram enter into an agreement - called the Covenant
between the Pieces - and God promises to make Avram's offspring
as numerous as the stars in the sky. Meanwhile, Sarai gives her
servant Hagar to Avram, and Hagar gives birth to Avram's first
son, Ishmael. This birth creates tension between Sarai and
Hagar.

God and Avram then enter into a second covenant. This covenant
involves circumcision. As part of the process Avram becomes
Avraham and Sarai becomes Sara.

This is the way the Torah tells the story of the split between Avram and Lot. See if you can figure out the real reason for this split.

And Avram went up from Egypt, he and his wife and all that was,
     and Lot with him to the Negev.
And Avram was very rich in cattle, in silver, and in gold.
And he journeyed by stages from the Negev as far as Beth-El
     as far as the place where his tent had been at the first -
     between Beth-El and Ai,
     to the place where he had built the first altar.
There Avram called out the name of the Lord.

And also Lot (who went with Avram) had sheep, oxen and tents.
And the land could not bear them to settle together,
     because their possessions were many -
     they were not able to settle together.
And there was a quarrel between the herdsmen of Avram's cattle
     and the herdsmen of Lot's cattle.
<u>And the Canaanites and the Perizzites were then settled in the
     land.</u>
And Avram said to Lot: "Let there not be quarreling between me
     and you, between my herdsmen and your herdsmen.
Because we are men-brothers.
Is not the whole land before you?
Please separate yourself from me.
If you to the left - I will to the right
If you to the right - I will to the left."
And Lot lifted up his eyes and saw all the plain of the Jordan,
     that all of it was a well watered plain,
     (before the Lord brought ruin upon Sodom and Gomorra)
     like the Garden of the Lord, like the land of Egypt (to
     where you come to Zoar).
And Lot chose for himself the whole plain of the Jordan,
And Lot journeyed eastward, and they separated themselves:
A man from his brother.   Gen. 13:1-11

1. Why is there a quarrel between Avram's and Lot's shepherds?
_____

_____

_____

2. When you read this story in the Torah, what is strange about
the line: "<u>and the Canaanites and the Perizzites were then
settled in the land.</u>"
_____

_____

_____

A MIDRASH: (GEN R. 41.6)

When Avram and Lot returned from Egypt, both of them had lots of
sheep and cattle. Avram was very careful about his sheep and
cattle, so he had them muzzled so that they would not eat from
fields where they weren't welcome. Avram knew that allowing his
flocks and herds to graze on someone else's fields was a kind of
robbery. Lot didn't muzzle his cattle and sheep. He felt that
it was too much bother, and he didn't really worry about what
his animals ate. Avram told Lot: "It is wrong not to muzzle
your flocks and herds - it is the same thing as stealing. This
land belongs to the Canaanites and the Perizzites. These fields
are theirs." Lot said to Avram: "If it is stealing - we are
stealing from ourselves. God has already promised this land to
us - there is no problem in our using it now."

Avram decided not to continue the argument. For the sake of
shalom bayit he let the matter drop. Later the argument was
picked up by the herdsmen. Lot's herdsmen said: "You are
really stupid - doing all that extra work - putting on and
taking off muzzles." Avram's herdsmen answered: "You are no
better than thieves." Lot's men answered: If we are stealing,
it is only from ourselves. Avram has no son. After he is dead
the land will belong to Lot. We are just using some of it now."

When Avram heard this, he decided that it was time to separate.

A. Underline the parts of this midrash which are taken directly
from the Torah?

B. How does the midrash explain the fight between the herdsmen?

_____
_____
_____

C. What is the message of this midrash?

_____
_____
_____

VAYERA is a sidra which continues with Avraham's adventures. The action opens with Avraham sitting in the doorway of his tent and seeing three strangers appear. He welcomes them and provides hospitality. They then inform him that Sara will give birth to a son. Sara laughs at this, God intercedes, and the son to be born is pre-named Yitzchak (from laughter).

God then informs Avraham that Sodom is to be destroyed because of its wickedness. Avraham argues with God and talks God into doing the <u>JUST</u> thing. God agrees to save the city if ten righteous people can be found (unfortunately they can't be found). God sends the angels in to rescue Lot and family.

Again it is time for there to be a famine in the land. This time Avraham and Sara go to Abimelech in Gerar. There they replay the wife-sister routine.

Finally, Yitzchak is born and a party is thrown. At this point tensions continue to mount between Sarah and Hagar and God tells Avraham to send Hagar and Ishmael off. They leave, and are rescued in the wilderness by an angel.

The sidra ends with the story of the binding of Yitzchak - a test where God asks Avraham to sacrifice his son Yitzchak. At the last moment an angel stops Avraham from completing the command.

At the beginning of this sidra, Avraham welcomes three
strangers. This is the way the Torah tells that story. As you
read it, see if you can figure out why Avraham was sitting in
front of his tent - almost looking for visitors.

The Lord appeared to him by the oaks of Mamre
        as he was sitting in the entrance of the tent at the heat
        of the day.
Looking up, he saw three men standing near him.
As soon as he saw them, he ran from the entrance to greet them,
        and bowed to the earth.
He said:"My lords, if I have found favor in your eyes - do not
        pass your servant by.
Let a little water be brought, then bathe your feet and recline
        under a tree.
I will bring you a little bread and you will refresh yourselves,
        and then you can continue on, seeing as you have come your
        servant's way."

They said: "Do as you have said."
Avraham ran to the oxen, took a young ox, tender and good, and
gave it to the boy, so that he should hasten to make it ready.
Then he took cream and milk and the young oxen that he had made
ready, and set it before them.
And he waited on them under the tree as they ate.

                                              Gen. 18:1-8

1. Why was Avraham sitting in front of his tent?

   _____

   _____

   _____

A MIDRASH (Gen R. 54.6)

Avraham lived in Beer-sheva for many years. He planted a garden there - and made it with four gates - facing north, south, east and west - and he planted a vineyard. No matter which direction a visitor would come from, there was always a gate facing him. The visitor would come into the garden, sit in the grove and eat and drink until he was satisfied. The house of Avraham was always open to all - and they came daily to eat and drink there. If one was hungry - Avraham gave him food and drink. If one was naked - Avraham provided a choice of garments and even provided him with silver and gold.

MIDRASH (Gen R. 48.8-9)

The day after the circumcision of Avraham,*God bore a hole down to the core of the earth so that the heat might fill the earth and so that no strangers would be wandering the roads and so Avraham would be left undisturbed in his pain. But the lack of strangers upset Avraham and he sent Eliezer his servant to look for them. When the servant returned with no results, Avraham, inspite of his weakness and pain, prepared to go out and look for those in need of hospitality.

A. Underline the parts of these midrashim which are based on facts found in the Torah.

B. How do these midrashim explain why Avraham is sitting in the door of his tent?

_____

_____

_____

C. What is the message of these midrashim?

_____

_____

_____

_____

_____

*If you look at the last thing which happened in LECH LECHA you will notice that Avraham was circumcised. The rabbis connected it to the beginning of VAYERA.

CHIYE SARA means the life of Sara and this is the sidra in which
Sara dies. In this sidra, Avraham goes into a long series of
business negotiations with Efron the Hittite. He purchases the
cave of the Machpelah which is used for the burial of all of the
patriarchs and matriarchs except Rachel. Sara is buried in the
cave.

Then, Avraham sends his servant Eliezer back to the city of
Nachor to find a wife for Yitzchak. There, at the well he meets
Rivka, the daughter of Bituel - a distant relative of Avraham.
He brings her back to Canaan and she and Yitzchak fall instantly
in love. Yitzchak brings her into his mother's tent and the two
begin their married life.

Meanwhile Avraham remarries and has a few more children. At the
end of the sidra he dies, and is buried in the cave of the
Machpelah by Yitzchak and Ishmael.

In this sidra it is made clear that Rivka is the right wife for
Yitzchak. As you read these sections from the Torah: (1) Find
the conditions Eliezer sets for finding the right woman. (2)
Decide what makes these conditions the right ones for finding
Yitzchak's wife. And (3) See if you can figure out why Yitzchak
feels that Rivka is the right woman?

And he said:
"God of my Master Avraham
      grant me good fortune today
      and show kindness to my master Avraham.
I am standing by the well
      and the daughters of the townspeople come to draw water -
Let it come to pass that the maiden to whom I say:
'Please lower your jar so I may drink,'
And she replies: 'Drink and I will also water your camels,'
Let her be the one you have decreed for your servant Yitzchak."

When he had just finished speaking
Rivka, who was born to Betuel, the son of Milcah the wife of
      Avraham's brother Nachor -
      came out with her jar on her shoulder.
The maiden was very beautiful -
      a virgin whom no man had known.
She went down to the well, filled her jar and came up.
Then the servant ran toward her and said: "Please let me sip a
      little water from your jar."
She said: "Drink my Lord." She quickly lowered her jar upon her
      hand and let him drink.When she had let him drink his fill,
      she said: "I will also draw water for your camels, until
      they finish drinking."
                        Gen: 24:12-20

And Yitzchak went out walking in the field toward evening
      and looking up he saw camels approaching.
Raising her eyes - Rivka saw Yitzchak.
She got off the camel and said to the servant:
"Who is that man walking in the field toward us?"
And the servant said: "That is my master."
So she took her veil and covered herself.
The servant told Yitzchak all these things which he had done.
Yitzchak then brought her into the tent of his mother Sara
      and he took Rivka as his wife.
Yitzchak loved her and thus found comfort after his mother's
      death.
                  Gen. 24:62-67

1. What was Eliezer's condition for finding the right wife?

_____

_____

2. Why was this a good condition?

_____

_____

3. How did Yitzchak know that she was the right woman?

_____

_____

A MIDRASH (Gen. R. 57.1)

When Eliezer saw a beautiful woman coming towards the well with a jug on her shoulder - he saw her stop beside a crying child. The child had cut his foot on a sharp stone. She washed and bound the wound and told the child: "Do not worry - it will soon heal." Then a half-blind woman had come to the well to draw water. Rivka helped her carry the full pitcher of water home. When Rivka returned, Eliezer asked her, "Will you give me a little water to drink?"

A MIDRASH (Gen. R. 60.7/Cf Zohar 1.113a)

Yitzchak took Rivka to the tent of his mother Sara, and she showed herself to be Sara's worthy successor. The cloud which was always over the tent during Sara's life was again visible. Again the tent glowed with light. When Sara was alive, she would light Shabbat candles and the glow would last the whole week, this too happened with Rivka. The blessing returned with Rivka and hovered over the tent.

A. Underline the parts of these midrashim which are based on facts or statements in the Torah.

B. Why do these midrashim think that Rivka was the right woman to be Yitzchak's wife?

_____

_____

_____

TOLDOT is a parasha which is mainly concerned with the struggles between Ya'akov and Esav.

At the beginning of the sidra, Rivka has a difficult time getting pregnant. Yitzchak prays to God and Rivka becomes pregnant with twins. The two children struggle in her womb causing her a great deal of pain. When the two are finally born, Esav is the first born, but Ya'akov is grabbing at his heel.

When the two children are grown, Ya'akov convinces Esav to sell him the birthright of the first born for a bowl of lentils. Then the focus shifts to Yitzchak. Again there is a famine in the land, and Yitzchak brings the family down to Gerar to Abimelech - again we have a wife-sister story. There is then a series of conficts over the right to wells which Avraham had dug.

When Yitzchak felt old, he sent for Esav, and told him to prepare for his blessing. Rivka overheard this and prepared Ya'akov to steal the blessing. Ya'akov fools his father and receives his brother's blessing. When Esav returns, Yitzchak gives him a blessing too.

At the end of the Torah portion we are given 2 reasons why Ya'akov should leave for Paddan-aram (the old country). Reason # 1: Esav wants to kill him. Reason # 2: Rivka doesn't want him to marry a Canaanite woman.

Here is the way the Torah tells the story of Ya'akov stealing the blessing. Read it carefully. Decide if you think Yitzchak really believed he was blessing Esav.

He went to his father and said: "Father."
And he said: "Hineini. Which of my sons are you?"
Ya'akov said to his father: "I am Esav, your first born.
     I have done as you have told me
     Pray sit and eat of my game
     so that your soul can bless me."
Yitzchak said to his son: "How did you succeed so quickly my
     son?"
And he said: "Because the Lord your God granted me good
     fortune."
Yitzchak said to Ya'akov: "Come closer that I might feel you my
     son - whether you are really my son Esav or not."
So Ya'akov came close to his father Yitzchak.
He felt him and said: "The voice is the voice of Ya'akov, but
     the hands are the hands of Esav."
He did not recognize him because his hands were hairy like those
     of his brother Esav.
And so he blessed him:
He asked: "Are you really my son Esav?"
And when he said: "I am," he said:
"Serve me and let me eat of my son's game that I may give you my
     soul's blessing."
So he served him and he ate, and he brought wine and he drank.
Then his father Yitzchak said to him: "Come close and kiss me my
     son."
He came close and kissed him and he smelled his clothes and
blessed him:
     See, the smell of my son
     is as the smell of the field
     which the Lord has blessed.
     May God give you
     of the dew of heaven and of the fat of the earth
     an abundance of new grain and wine.
     People will serve you
     Nations will bow to you
     Be master over your brother
     And let your mother's sons bow to you.
     Those who curse you will be cursed
     Those who bless you will be blessed

                                                    Gen. 27:18-29

Do you think Ya'akov really fooled Yitzchak? Bring evidence from the text.

_____

_____

_____

A MIDRASH (Tanchuma Toldot 8)

Esav's marriage with the daughters of Canaan upset Yitzchak as much as it did Rivka. In fact he suffered more at this daughters-in-law's hands. It was their fault that he lost his sight and became old so quickly. His daughters-in-law began to burn incense to their idols both day and night. Rivka was used to the smoke from the incense, because she had been raised in a hom which worshiped idols. Yitzchak had never experienced this before. Both the smoke form the incense and the presence of the idols hurt him.

A MIDRASH (Gen. R. 65.19-23)

Ya'akov entered the tent and called to Yitzchak: "Father." Yitzchak answered: "Hineini." When his father asked: "Which one are you my son?" Ya'akov carefully phrased his answer. He said: "It is I, Esav is your first born." This way he didn't lie, even though he did mislead his father. When Yitzchak asked how the work had been completed so quickly, Ya'akov said: "Because the Lord your God granted me good fortune." Yitzchak realized that this wasn't Esav because Esav would never have mentioned the name of God.

A. Underline the "facts" and "quotations" from the Torah this midrash uses?

B. What does this midrash teach us about (1) Esav, and (2) why it was okay for Ya'akov to steal the blessing?

_____
_____
_____
_____
_____
_____

C. What is the message of this midrash?

_____
_____
_____
_____
_____
_____

A. Underline the "facts" and "quotations" from the Torah which this midrash uses.

B. According to this midrash, did Ya'akov fool Yitzchak?

_____
_____
_____
_____
_____
_____
_____
_____
_____

C. What is the moral of this midrash?

_____
_____
_____
_____
_____
_____
_____

VAYETZE is the parasha where Ya'akov comes into his own. It
begins with his leaving home and stopping to sleep at Beth El.
There he has a dream of angels going up and down on a ladder.

When he arrives in Nachor, he meets Rachel and falls in love.
He discovers that she is the daughter of Lavan his relative. He
works out a deal to work for seven years in order to marry her.
At the end of the seven years, Lavan substitutes Leah, his older
daughter. Ya'akov is forced to work another seven years for
Rachel.

Then Leah and Rachel enter into battle of the births. They have
a contest to see who could provide Ya'akov with the most
children. Leah gives birth to Reuven, Shimon, Levi and Yehuda.
Then Rachel had her maid Bilha mother sons: Dan and Naphtali.
To stay in the competition, Leah enters her maid Zilpah who
gives birth to Gad and Asher. Then Leah mothers Yissachar,
Zevulun and a daughter Dina. Finally, Rachel gives birth to
Yosef.

Finally Ya'akov prepares to leave Lavan. They work out a deal
on what of the flock will be Ya'akov's. With all his
possessions in hand, he leaves with his family. However, he
didn't know that Rachel had stolen the family idols. Lavan
chases him to retreive the idols, but doesn't find them.

The sidra ends with the family returning to Caanan and being met
by angels.

Here is the way the Torah describes the wedding in which Ya'akov
expected to marry Rachel and wound up with Leah. As you read
it, see if you can figure out how he was fooled:

Then Ya'akov said to Lavan:
"Give me my wife - for my time is completed
    that I may consort with her."
And Lavan gathered all the people of the place
    and made a feast.
And it came to pass in the evening
    that he took his daughter Leah and brought her to him
    and he cohabitated with her.
And Lavan had given his maid servant Zilpah to his daughter Leah
    as a maid -
And it came to pass in the morning - hinei Leah.
And he said to Lavan: "What is this you have done to me?
Was it not for Rachel that I served you?
Why did you deceive me?"

                                    Gen: 29:21-25

How could Lavan fool Ya'akov? Couldn't Ya'kov tell that he had
the wrong woman?

_____

_____

_____

_____

A MIDRASH (Megillah 13a)

The Talmud records this conversation between Ya'akov and Rachel
Ya'akov: "Do you want to marry me?"
Rachel: "Yes, but my father is a swindler and he will cheat
      you."
Ya'akov: "Do not worry, I know how to trick him back."
Rachel: "Is a Tzadik allowed to cheat?"
Ya'akov: "If the person with whom he is dealing is a cheat - one
      is allowed to outwit him. But what fraud does he intend to
      pull?"
Rachel: "I have an older sister. He will try to switch me for
      her."
Ya'akov: "If so, let us now work out signs by which I will know
      that it is really you."

A MIDRASH (GEN. R. 71.18/Petichta of Eicha R.)

When Leah was about to be presented as the bride, Rachel
thought, "I can't allow my sister to be shamed in public."
She added: "If I have not been found worthy to build up the
Jewish people, let my sister do it." She then told her the
secret signs. She even hid in the room where the couple were
staying and answered Ya'akov's questions so that Leah's voice
would not give her away.

A MIDRASH (GEN. R. 70.19)

The morning after the wedding night, Ya'akov said to Leah:
"You are the daughter of a deceiver and a cheat. Why did you
answer "Hineini" everytime I called Rachel's name?"
She answered him: "Is there a teacher who doesn't have a
student? I learned from you. When your father called you Esav
- you answered: 'Hineini.'"

**A. Underline the parts of these midrashim which are taken
directly from the Torah.**

B. How do these midrashim explain how Ya'akov was fooled?
_____
_____
_____

C. What are the morals of the last two midrashim?
_____
_____
_____
_____

VAYISHLACH begins on the eve of Ya'akov's reunion with Esav. He sends messagers ahead to greet Esav, then he divides his people and herds into two camps. He also prepares gifts for Esav.

On the night before the meeting, Ya'akov is left alone, and he wrestles with a man (who might be an angel) until dawn was breaking. At the end of the struggle, Ya'akov has a hurt leg, but the other wrestler is unable to escape. When he demands to be released, Ya'akov demands a blessing. The wrestling partner changes his name from Ya'akov (the heel) to Yisrael (the Godwrestler).

In the morning, Ya'akov and Esav meet, and an understanding of living in peace is worked out between the brothers. After the meeting Ya'akov moves to Shechem. There, Dinah, his daugher with Leah, gets involved with a man named Shechem. Simon and Levi destroy the city of Shechem as a way of getting revenge.

Next, Ya'akov goes to Beth-El and builds an altar. There, God appears to him and blesses him: again changing his name from Ya'akov to Yisrael. After the blessing, Rachel dies in childbirth. Her son is named Binyamin, and she is buried on the road.

The sidra ends with an incident between Reuven and Bilhah, a listing of Ya'akov's twelve sons, the death of Yitzchak (who is buried in the Cave of the Machpelah by Ya'akov and Esav) and a long geneology of Esav's children.

This is the way the Torah tells the story of Rachel's death and burial. Read it closely. See if you can figure out why Rachel was the only one of the patriarchs and matriarchs who wasn't buried in the cave of the Machpelah?

They set out from Bethel
but when they were still a distance from Efrat
Rachel gave birth
and had a hard delivery.
It came to pass
when the delivery was going hardest
that the midwife said to her:
"Be not afraid
for it is another son for you."
As she was breathing her last breath
(for she was dying)
she called his name: Binoni (son of my woe)
but his father called him: Binyamin (son of the right hand)
Rachel died.
She was buried on the road to Efrat —
now Bethlehem.
Ya'akov set up a pillar
Today that pillar is still Rachel's buring place   Gen: 35:16-20

Why do you think that Rachel was buried outside of Bethlehem?

_____

_____

A MIDRASH (Gen. R. 84.2)

When Yosef was being carried into slavery, the caravan passed Rachel's tomb. Yosef threw himself on the ground and cried: "Mother, Mother - your son has been taken from his father and sold into slavery." He hugged the stones and cried. A voice came up from inside the tomb: "I know of your suffering my son, but do not be afraid to go to Egypt. God is with you and will protect you."

A MIDRASH (Pesikta Rabbati 3:69)

Before he died, Ya'akov explained to Yosef: "I really wanted to bury your mother in the cave of the Machpelah, but God ordered her buried at the crossroads of Bethlehem. She was placed there to give comfort to B'nai Yisrael when they are carried away into the Babylonian exile. She will plead to God, God will listen to her prayers and B'nai Yisrael will indeed return from that exile." This indeed came to pass in 586 B.C.E.

A. Underline the parts of these midrashim which can be found in the Bible. (Hints: For the first midrash - look at Genesis 46.3-4, for the second midrash, know that the bible has a long description of the Babylonian exile and return.

B. What stories do these midrashim add to the Torah?

_____
_____
_____

C. According to these midrashim, why was Rachel buried outside of Bethlehem?

_____
_____

D. What do these midrashim teach about Jewish history?

_____
_____
_____

VAYESHEV is the sidra which begins the Yosef story. It starts when Yosef is 17 years old. (Remember that number, see if you can find where it pops up again). Yosef has a poor relationship with his brothers (except for Binyamin) because he was his father's favorite. Yisrael had a special coat made for him. He has two dreams, one about sheaves of grain in the fields and the other about the heavens. Both of these dreams show the whole family bowing down to Yosef. This made the brothers hate him more.

Now the plot thickens. Yisrael sends Yosef out to join his brothers in the field. The brothers rip off his special coat and throw him in a pit. They sell him to traders who eventually sell him to Potifar in Egypt.

Before the Yosef story continues, we have a short story about Judah, his son Onan, and a side adventure between Judah and Tamar.

Then, the parasha returns to Egypt where Yosef makes good in the house of Potifar, but is then thrown in prison when Potifar's wife invents a story about Yosef seducing her.

In prison, he meets two of Pharaoh's servants, a butler and a baker, both of whom Pharaoh had thrown in prison. Both of these men have dreams and Yosef interprets them. He tells the butler that he will be returned to Pharoah's service, and he tells the baker that he will be executed. His interpretation comes true.

This is the Torah's story of the butler and the baker whom Yosef meets in prison. As you read the story, see if you can figure out why the butler is saved and the baker is executed.

It came to pass after these things
that the butler of the king of Egypt
and the baker
sinned against their lord - the king of Egypt.

Pharaoh was angry with his two officials...
and put them in custody at the same prison where Yosef was kept.

They remained in custody many days.
And the two of them dreamed a dream on the same night.
Each had his own dream and his own meaning.

The chief of butlers told his dream to Yosef.
He said to him:
Hinei - a vine was before me
On the vine were three branches.
It had barely budded but out came blossoms
 and its clusters ripened into grapes.
Pharaoh's cup was in my hand
and I took the grapes and pressed them into Pharaoh's cup
and I give the cup into Pharaoh's hand.

Yosef said to him:
This is its interpretation:
The three branches are three days.
In another three days Pharaoh will parden you and restore you to your post.
And you will give Pharaoh's cup into his hand.

When the baker saw that he had interpreted for good,
He said to Yosef: I too had a dream.
Hinei three baskets of white bread were on my head
and in the top basket were all kinds of food for Pharaoh - a good baker's work.
And the birds eat out of the basket from my head.
Yosef answered him:
The three baskets are three days.
Pharaoh will lift off your head in three days...

And it came about on the third day...   Gen: 40:1-20

In your opinion, why was the butler returned to power and the baker put to death?

_____

_____

_____

A MIDRASH (Midrash Lekach Tov)

Both the butler and the baker had seemed to do their jobs
poorly. The butler handed Pharaoh a goblet of wine with a fly
in it. The baker had delivered bread with splinters of wood in
it. Eventually Pharaoh's counselors figured out the difference.
The butler's error could have been an honest mistake - he could
have poured the cup carefully, but a fly could have landed in it
at the last moment. The baker's mistake was clearly a careless
one. If he had sifted the flour carefully, there was no way for
splinters to get in the bread. The baker was responsible for
his negligence. Therefore, the baker was hanged while the
butler was returned to his duties.

**A. Underline the parts of this midrash which are based on facts
found in the biblical text.**

**B. How does this midrash explain why the butler was saved and
the baker was killed?**

_____

_____

_____

**C. Do you think there is a message being taught by this
midrash? If so, what is the moral?**

_____

_____

_____

MIKETZ continues the story of Yosef. (When we left Yosef last sidra, he was in prison). Meanwhile, Pharaoh has two dreams which no one can interpret. The butler finally remembers Yosef, tells Pharoah about his ability to interpret dreams, and Yosef is taken from prison. He successfully explains that Pharaoh's two dreams warn that there will be seven years of plenty followed by seven years of famine. Pharaoh puts Yosef in charge of preparing Egypt for the famine. Yosef takes an Egyptian wife - Osnat and she gives him two sons: Efraim and Manashe.

Seven years of plenty come to pass, and now there is famine. Back in Canaan, Ya'akov sends ten of his sons (but not Binyamin) down to Egypt to buy food. When they get to Egypt, they are forced to buy food from Yosef, a man whom they don't recognize. He gives them a hard time and even accuses them of being spies. In the end, he gives them sacks of grain, hides their money in the sacks, and warns them that if they return for more food, they must bring Binyamin with them.

The famine of course, continues, and the brothers are forced to return to Egypt. After a long bargaining session, Yisrael agrees to let Binyamin go. When they arrive in Egypt, Yosef invites them to a banquet. (At one point he starts to cry, but hides his tears from the brothers). This time, he hides a goblet in Binyamin's pack. The sidra ends with Binyamin being caught, and with his fate still unknown.

This is the Torah's explanation of how Yosef distributed grain during the famine. As you read it, see if you can figure out what principles he was using to distribute the grain.

During the seven years of plenty - the land produced in handfuls.
And he gathered all the grain in Egypt during the seven years
And he stored the grain in the cities
each city stored the grain from the fields around it.
Yosef stored up corn like the sand of the sea
very much - more than could be counted

The seven years of plenty in the land of Egypt came to an end.
and the seven years of famine began
just as Yosef had said.
Famine was in all lands
but in all the land of Egypt there was bread.
Now when all the land of Egypt was hungry
and the people went to Pharaoh for bread
Pharaoh said to all the Egyptians:
"Go to Yosef, whatever he tells you - you shall do
The famine spread over the whole face of the earth
Yosef opened all that was within and rationed out grain to the Egyptians
And the famine became stronger in the land of Egypt
And from all lands they came to the land of Egypt -
to Yosef - to buy grain
for the famine was strong in all lands

Gen. 41:47-57

What was behind Yosef's plan for distributing grain?

_____

_____

_____

_____

A MIDRASH (Gen. R. 91.4)

Yosef introduced these laws for the distribution of food:
   * Not only Egyptians but any hungry people can buy grain.
   * A master must come and buy the food for his household -
     a slave cannot be sent.
   * No one will be sold more grain than can be carried on one
donkey.
   * Food may only be bought for personal use, anyone trying
     to make a profit will be put to death.
   * The names of anyone buying grain from outside of Egypt
       will be recorded.

The Egyptians thought that Yosef did all of this to be fair and
just. Little did they know that he had other reasons. Yosef
was sure that his brothers would need to come to Egypt to buy
food and this would let him locate his father. Since slaves
could not be sent, and since no one could carry more than one
donkey's worth of grain, Yisrael had to send the whole family.
In addition, the recording of names made sure that Yosef could
locate them.

In the past, food was only distributed to Egyptians, Yosef saw
to it that all who were hungry could buy food. This was an
intentional act of <u>Chesed</u> by Yosef.

A.   On what facts in the Torah are these midrashim based?
_____
_____
_____

B.   What new rules for distributing grain do these midrashim
introduce?
_____
_____
_____

C.   What two different explanations of these rules are given?
_____
_____

D.   What value is being taught here? (If you look closely, you
may find a second value)
_____
_____

VAYIGASH brings us to the conclusion of the Yosef story. When
last we left the brothers, Yosef was going to keep Binyamin for
a slave (after framing him with a goblet). This sidra opens
with Yehuda pleading for Binyamin and even offering to remain in
his place. At this point Yosef begins to cry, and reveals
himself to his brothers.

Pharaoh is informed that Yosef's brothers have come to Egypt and
he welcomes them and the rest of the family in Egypt. The
brothers return, inform Ya'akov that his son Yosef is still
alive, and Ya'akov decides to go to Egypt.

Yisrael offers sacrifices in Beersheva, sees God in a vision,
and then goes down to Egypt. They settle in the land of Goshen.

The sidra ends with Pharaoh meeting Ya'akov and family, and then
goes into a detailed description of how Yosef ran the grain
business during the famine.

This passage tells how the brothers told their father Yisrael that Yosef was still alive. Read the text and see if you can figure out why he finally believes them.

Then he sent his brothers on their way,
as they went he said to them:
"Do not fight along the way."
They went up from Egypt
and came to the land of Canaan
to Ya'akov their father
And they told him, saying: "Yosef is still alive,
indeed, he is ruler of all the land of Egypt."
His heart went numb for he did not believe them.
Then they spoke to him all the words which Yosef had spoken to them.
He saw the wagons which Yosef had sent to carry him.
And the spirit of their father lived again.
Yisrael said: "Enough! My son Yosef is still alive!
I will go and see him before I die." Gen. 45:24-28

What do you think finally convinced Yisrael that Yosef was indeed alive?

_____

_____

_____

_____

33

A MIDRASH (Yalkut: Aleph 152, Gen R. 94.5, and other sources)

Yosef told his brothers to tell Yaakov the following: "When we left Egypt, Yosef insisted on escorting us, because the last **halacha** you taught him was the law of escorting a guest." At first Ya'akov did not believe the brothers, but when they told him all that Yosef had done, including his message about the **halacha** – Ya'akov finally believed them. He said: "Yosef is still alive," but he also meant "Yosef is still a tzadik."

Ya'akov was happier to find that his son was still a tzadik than he was to discover that he was a king.

A. Underline the parts of this story which are also found in the Torah text.

B. According to this midrash, what caused Ya'akov to believe that Yosef was still alive?

_____
_____
_____

C. What is the message of this midrash?

_____
_____
_____

VAYECHI brings to an end, the stories of Yosef and Ya'akov. At the beginning of the parasha, Ya'akov sends for Yosef and makes him swear that Yosef will not bury him in Egypt, but rather will have his body returned to the cave of the Machpelah in Canaan.

Ya'akov blesses Yosef's two sons: Efraim and Manashe - blessing the younger in the place of the older. Then Ya'akov blesses each of the 12 sons. These are now the 12 tribes of Yisrael.

Ya'akov dies after living 17 years in Egypt (remember the number 17) and Yosef fulfills his wishes, buring him in Canaan. After Ya'akov's death, the brothers are fearful that Yosef will now take revenge - but he reassures them that all is forgiven.

The sidra ends (ending the book of BERESHIT) with Yosef's death. He is enbalmed and buried in Egypt. Before his death, he made B'nai Yisrael swear to bring his bones up to Canaan from Egypt.

CHAZAK CHAZAK V'NITCHAZEK

Just before Ya'akov dies, he brings his sons together for a blessing. There seems to be something different about this blessing - different from other blessings we have seen. As you read this Torah text, see if you can figure out (1) what is different about these blessings, and (2) what Ya'akov is trying to communicate.

And Ya'akov called his sons together and said to them:
Join together so I may tell you
what will happen to you in the days to come

Gather together and listen B'nai Ya'akov
listen to Yisrael your father

Reuven - you are my first born...
You brought disgrace - mounting my couch

Shimon and Levi - the brothers
I will divide them in Ya'akov
I will scatter them in Yisrael

Yehuda - your brothers will praise you

Zevulun - on the sea shore he dwells

Yissachar - a bony ass - becoming a toiling serf

Dan - will be a serpant by the wayside

Gad shall be raided by raiders

Asher will have rich bread

Naftali - a hind let loose

Yosef - a wild ass - elect of his brothers

Binyamin - a wolf which tears to pieces   Gen. 49:1-27

1. What is different about this blessing?

_____

_____

_____

2. What is Ya'akov trying to tell his sons?

_____

_____

_____

A MIDRASH (Tanchuma, Vayechi 11)

Ya'akov was afraid that God's presence had left him because his sons were unworthy of a Divine blessing. He therefore asked his sons: "How do I know if your hearts are full with God's will?"

All of B'nai Yisrael answered him: **Sh'ma Yisrael Hashem Elohenu Hashen Echad** - Listen Yisrael - The Lord our God. The Lord alone. Ya'akov bowed in thanks to God and quietly answered: **Baruch Shem K'vod l'olam va'ed.** Then he blessed B'nai Yisrael - his 12 sons.

A. What words in the text hint that the SH'MA might first have been said at this moment in history.

_____

_____

B. According to the midrash, what fear was behind these blessings?

_____

_____

_____

C   What does this midrash teach us about the SH'MA?

_____

_____

_____

SHEMOT begins the story of the Exodus from Egypt. At the end of
the book of Genesis, we left B'nai Yisrael, all 70 of them, in
Egypt. As the book of Exodus begins, a whole number of changes
has taken place. Yosef and all his generation have died, and
B'nai Yisrael have multiplied from a family to a nation. A new
king arose over Egypt who didn't know about Yosef and his
special relationship.

The new Pharaoh begins a 5 point process of persecution which
includes: taskmasters, enslavement, bitter oppression, having
the midwives kill male children, and then ordering all the
people to do the same.

Next, Moshe is born, set afloat on the Nile, and then adopted by
Pharaoh's daughter. When he has grown, he kills a taskmaster
who was beating a Hebrew slave and then flees from Egypt.

Moshe flees to Midian, saves the daughters of the local priest
Yitro, and marries one of them - Tzipora. They have a son named
Gershon. Moshe becomes a shepherd, and one day while tending
the flocks by Mt. Sinai, he sees a burning bush and talks with
God. After a long dialogue, he is given orders to return to
Egypt and release the Jewish people from slavery.

CONTINUED

Moshe begins his mission. He bids Yitro farewell and has an
encounter with God over the fact that Gershon was not
circumcised. He joins with his brother Aharon and they present
their demands to Pharaoh to 'Let their people go.' Pharaoh
reacts by making the Hebrews now bake their bricks without
straw. B'nai Yisrael blames Moshe and Aharon for the harder
work.

After Moshe fled from Egypt, he came to Midian and became a
shepherd. The Torah only tells this short story about his
experience as a shepherd. As you read, see if you can decide
(1) why it was important training for Moshe to be a shepherd,
and (2) why he lead his flock all the way from Midian to Mount
Horeb (a.k.a. Mount Sinai).

Now Moshe tended the flock of his father-in-law Yitro
the priest of Midian.
He drove the flock to the farthest end of the wilderness
and came to the mountain of the God to Horev
And the angel of the Lord appeared to him
in a flame of fire out of the midst of the bush
And he looked
and hinei
the bush burned with fire but was not burned up.
And Moshe said: "I must turn aside to look at this marvelous
     sight. Why is this bush not burnt up?"
And when the Lord saw that he had turned aside to look -
God called to him out of the midst of the bush: "Moshe, Moshe."
And he answered: "Hineini."

                                              Ex. 3.1-4

1. Why do you think it was "good for Moshe" to spend time as a
shepherd?

_____

_____

_____

2. Why would Moshe take his flock as far as Sinai? (A HINT:
Think about what Avraham did with his sheep)

_____

_____

_____

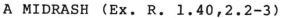

A MIDRASH (Ex. R. 1.40,2.2-3)

As soon as Moshe took over Yitro's flocks they were blessed. Not a single animal was ever injured by a wild beast. Moshe used to graze his flocks in ownerless land to insure that they would not steal from lands which were not Yitro's.

Once a lamb ran away from the flock. Moshe followed it until it reached some bushes near a pond. It stopped to drink. Moshe said: "I didn't know you ran all this way because you were thirsty. You must be tired too." He lifted the lamb on his shoulder and carried it back to the flock.

A MIDRASH (Ibid 2.2)

God tested two people by making them shepherds. One of them was King David who used to protect the smaller sheep from the attacks of the larger ones, and who would make sure that each animal got the food which was best for it. God said: "A man who cares for the needs of each individual sheep will do the same for My people B'nai Yisrael."

Moshe was also tested. God said: "A man who tends sheep with such mercy will be a compassionate leader for My sheep, Yisrael."

A. Underline the parts of these midrashim which are based on facts in the Bible.

B. How do these midrashim explain why it was good for Moshe to be a shepherd?

_____

_____

_____

C. How do these midrashim explain why Moshe led his herd as far as Mt. Sinai?

_____

_____

_____

D. Be creative — use the idea of being a shepherd as good training to write your own midrash on why Moshe went to Mt. Sinai.

_____

_____

_____

_____

_____

_____

_____

_____

_____

_____

_____

E. What is the moral of your midrash?

_____

_____

F. What lessons are taught by the other two midrashim?

_____

_____

_____

_____

In this sidra, Moshe and Aharon go into action and begin to
organize the slave revolt. VA'ERA begins with God giving Moshe,
and then Moshe and Aharon a pep talk. Then the Torah lists the
major leaders of B'nai Yisrael. It is here that Moshe complains
about not being able to speak properly.

Moshe and Aharon go to Pharaoh and do the old staff into snake
trick. They ask Pharaoh to allow their people to go into the
wilderness to sacrifice to their God. Then they introduce the
first plague. Aharon holds his staff over the Nile river, and
all the water in Egypt is turned into blood. Pharaoh's heart
was hard and he didn't respond.

Next, Aharon holds out his staff over the canals and frogs fill
the land. This is the second plague. This time Pharaoh gives
in and the frogs are removed.

Pharaoh changes his mind and Aharon brings the third plague. He
struck the ground with his staff and lice filled the land.
Pharaoh's heart remains hardened.

Moshe goes to Pharaoh and warns that the land will be filled
with swarms of insects if Pharoah doesn't allow the people to go
into the wilderness to worship God. The Lord filled the land
with swarms of insects.

CONTINUED

Pharaoh sends for Moshe and Aharon and agrees to let B'nai
Yisrael go 3 days into the wilderness to worship. The swarms of
insects vanish. Afterwards, Pharaoh changes his mind and won't
let them go. Next God had all of the sheep and cattle in Egypt
die of the pestilence. Still Pharaoh won't let them go.

Next Moshe and Aharon take handfuls of soot, throw it in the
air, and boils began to break out on every Egyptian. But
Pharaoh's heart remained hardened and he would not let them go.

Next Moshe warned Pharaoh that the seventh plague would be hail.
He held out the staff to the sky and hail struck down people and
animals who were outside, and destroyed all the crops.

This parasha ends with Pharaoh's heart still hardened and with
him refusing to let the Jewish people go.

**This text is the Torah's version of how the first plague
happened. As you read it, see if you can figure out why Aharon
starts this plague rather than Moshe**

And the Lord said to Moshe:
   "Pharaoh's heart is hardened
   he refuses to let the people go
   Go to Pharaoh in the morning
   when he is coming out of the water
   you shall stand at the river bank to meet him
   and take in your hand the staff that turned into a snake.
   And you shall say to him: 'The Lord, the God of the Hebrews
   sent me to you to say: "Let My people go that they may
   worship me in the wilderness..."

And the Lord said to Moshe:
   "Say to Aharon: 'Take your rod and hold out your arm over
   the waters of Egypt - its rivers, its canals, its ponds,
   all its bodies of water - that they may turn to blood..."

                                              (Edited Ex. 7.14-19)

**Why do you think that Aharon was the one to bring the plague to
Egypt while Moshe gave the warning? (Remember, Aharon was
suposed to do the talking and Moshe the leading).**

_____

_____

_____

A MIDRASH (EX. R. 20.1)

Moshe repeated God's word to Pharaoh and warned him that the
Nile would turn to blood. When Pharaoh ignored the warning, God
ordered Moshe to strike the river and bring the plague. Moshe
objected: "How can I strike the Nile? Can someone who drank
from a well throw stones into it? As a baby I was saved by the
waters of the Nile - how can I strike these same waters?"

**A. Underline the parts of this midrash which can also be found
in the Torah.**

B. How does this midrash explain why Aharon brought this plague?
_____
_____
_____

C. What value does this midrash teach?
_____
_____
_____

Continuing with the adventures of the Exodus, we come to parshat
BO. So far, 7 of the 10 plagues have hit Egypt. We start with
the eighth plague. Again Moshe warns Pharaoh, the warning is
ignored, and Moshe holds up the staff and brings the locust
swarms.

Pharaoh sends for Moshe and Aharon, agrees to let B'nai Yisrael
go, then changes his mind once the plague is over.

God has Moshe hold out his staff and bring the nineth plague -
darkness. Pharaoh sends for Moshe, they fail to work out a
deal, and Moshe then follows God's order to warn them of the
10th plague - the death of the first born.

God then teaches Moshe the first mitzvah given to all of
Yisrael, the marking of the new month. This is then followed by
rules for the observance of the first Pesach. While these
seders are going on in homes marked with blood of the lambs on
the mezzuzot, the 10th plague, the death of the first born, hits
Egypt. At this point Pharaoh tries to rush B'nai Yisrael out of
Egypt.

At last the Exodus has begun. Before we finish the sidra
however, the Torah teaches rules about who can celebrate pesach
and rules about the mitzvah to sanctify the firstborn male of
both people and animals.

In the middle of the ten plagues, God introduces the first
mitzvot which are directly taught to Israel. Here is the way
the Torah presents these mitzvot. See if you can figure out (1)
Why fixing the calendar is an important first mitzvah, and (2)
why the month which contain's Pesach should be the first month -
rather than the month of Tishre - which has Rosh Hashana? Read
on.The Lord said to Moshe and Aharon in the land of Egypt:

"This month shall mark for you the beginning of months, it shall
be the first of the months of the year for you."

Speak to the whole congregation of Yisrael and say to them:
'On the tenth of this month each of them shall take a lamb...'

Ex. 12.1-3

1. Why would a mitzvah about a new month be the first
commandment taught to all of Yisrael?

_____

_____

2. How can Nissan be the first month, when the month of Tishre
has Rosh Hashana (the new year)?

_____

_____

_____

A MIDRASH (Ex. R. 15.10)

On the first of Nissan (the month of Pesach), God told Moshe
that this will be the first of all months in the Jewish
calendar.

To what can this be compared? This can be compared to a country
where the birthday of the King's son was a national holiday
every year. One day, when the prince was grown up, he visited a
foreign country and was taken prisoner for many years. Finally
he was released. The whole country celebrated his return. The
king ordered that from now on, the day the prince was set free
would be a national holiday rather than his birthday.

A. This midrash too is a parable. It too, is not directly based on any specific Torah text.

B. What do each of these represent:

The King_____

The Prince_____

The birthday_____

The liberation day_____

C. What is the moral message of this midrash?

_____

_____

A MIDRASH (Ex. R. 15:30)

God informed Moshe: "For 2,448 years I have proclaimed every new month in heaven, but now that you have become a nation - I give you the responsibility."

To what can this be compared? This can be compared to a King who carefully guarded the keys to his treasury and would allow no one to touch them. However as soon as the King's son came of age, the King gave him the keys.and said: "In the future you will be responsible for them."

A. None of this midrash is directly based on facts from the Torah. What question about the text is this midrash trying to answer?

_____

_____

B. This midrash is a parable. Figure out what each of the following represent:

The King_____

The Prince_____

The Key_____

C. What is the message of this midrash?

_____

_____

With parshat B'SHALLACH, B'nai Yisrael is off and running from Egypt. God leads them the long way avoiding the land of the Philistines. Meanwhile back in Egypt, Pharaoh has a change of heart and gives chase.

It is at the Yam Suf that Pharaoh catches B'nai Yisrael. God tells Moshe to stop praying and lift his staff. The sea divides and B'nai Yisrael crosses, but Pharaoh and his army are drowned when the sea closes.

On the other side of the sea, Moshe and B'nai Yisrael sing a song of praise - the song of the sea - to God. Miriam, Moshe and Aharon's sister also led the women in song and dance.

As soon as they move into the wilderness, the people begin to complain, so Moshe makes bitter water sweet to ease their complaints. God also introduces Manna - the special food which falls from the sky daily (except Shabbat). To complete the menu, God also sees to it that quail could be easily caught.

Before B'nai Yisrael can move even another chapter into the sidra, they again complain about the lack of water. Moshe follows God's instructions and hits a rock - bringing forth water.

To end this parasha, Joshua fights a battle with Amalek. Moshe Aharon and Hur go up on a hill. As long as Moshe can keep his arms in the air - B'nai Yisrael wins the battle...

At the edge of the Yam Suf, B'nai Yisrael sang a song of praise
to God. Read the text of part of this song. See if you can
find anything wrong with it. See if you can explain why it was
the right song for B'nai Yisrael to sing.

Then Moshe and B'nai Yisrael sang this song to the Lord
They said:

I will sing to the Lord for He has triumphed gloriously
Horse and driver He has thrown into the sea
The Lord is my strength and might
and He is become my salvation.
This is my God and I will sing to Him,
The God of my father and I will exalt Him
The Lord is a Warrior
Lord is His name
Pharaoh's Chariots and his army
He has cast into the sea,
and the pick of his officers
are drowned in the Yam Suf
The deep covers them
They went down into the depths like a stone
Your right hand Lord is glorious in power
Your right hand Lord shatters the foe.

                          Ex. 15.1-6

1. What might make this song a poor thing for Moshe and B'nai
Yisrael to sing?

_____

_____

2. What makes it the right thing to sing?

_____

_____

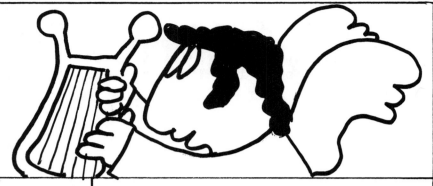

A MIDRASH (Ex. R. 23.8)

When the Egyptian army was
chasing B'nai Yisrael, the
angels in heaven wanted to sing
the song of the sea to God.
God would not let them. God
said: "How can you sing My
praises when B'nai Yisrael are
scared to death while crossing
the Yam Suf?"

After B'nai Yisrael had safely
crossed the sea, the angels
once again wanted to sing the
song of the sea. God still
said no. God told them: "How
can you sing when My creatures
are drowning? My mercy goes out
to all people."

A MIDRASH (Ex. R. 23.8)

Even though God prevented the
angels from singing the song of
the sea, B'nai Yisrael were
given permission to sing it.
God did this because B'nai
Yisrael had actually
experienced the miracles and
had the obligation to thank and
praise God for saving them.

**A.   Here we have two Midrashim which are based on a question about
the Torah. What is that question?**

_____

_____

**B.   According to the first midrash, what seems wrong with the
song of the sea?**

_____

_____

**C.   According to the second midrash, why was it right for B'nai
Yisrael to sing the song of the sea?**

_____

_____

**D.   These midrashim express two conflictiong values - what are
they?**

_____

_____

In sidrat YITRO, Yitro makes a return entrance. Moshe and B'nai
Yisrael are camped at Mount Sinai. Yitro, having heard of all
the wonders which have taken place in Egypt, takes Tzipora and
Gershom and brings them to Moshe. Yitro offers sacrifices to
God.

While he is around camp, Yitro sees how busy Moshe is - serving
as a judge for all the people. He suggests that Moshe set up a
series of judges. Moshe follows his suggestion.

God then presents B'nai Yisrael with a series of conditions for
a special event which is to take place. The ten commandments
are then given from Mount Sinai.

All the people witness the thunder and lightning, the smoking
mountain and the other effects and they were afraid. They ask
Moshe to serve as a go-between with God.

At the end of the sidra are two short laws: (1) Make no idols,
and (2) Use no stones in an altar which has been shaped by metal
tools.

This sidra has the 10 commandments given to B'nai Yisrael. Before the laws are given, there is a description of how God had selected B'nai Yisrael to be a chosen people. As you read this text, see if you can figure out why Mount Sinai was the chosen mountain.

On the third new moon after B'nai Yisrael had gone forth from the land of Egypt,
on that very day they entered the wilderness of Sinai.
Having journeyed from Refidim,
they entered the wilderness of Sinai
and encamped at the front of the mountain.
And Moshe went up to God.
And the Lord called to him from the mountain saying:
    "This you shall say to B'nai Yisrael.
    You have seen what I did to the Egyptians,
    how I bore you on eagles' wings
    and brought you to Me.
    Now then if you will obey My voice
    and keep My covenant,
    You shall be My treasure from among the peoples.
    All the earth is mine,
    but you shall be to Me a kingdom of priests and a holy nation.

Ex: 19:1-6

Why was Mount Sinai the right place for God to give the 10 commandments to B'nai Yisrael?

_____

_____

A MIDRASH (Gen. R. 79.1)

When God chose Mount Sinai to
be the place where the Torah
was given, a quarrel broke out
among the mountains. Each one
insisted that "The Torah should
have been given on me." Mount
Tavor and Mount Carmel both
claimed to be the right
mountain. God however told the
mountains - none of you is
right, because each of you
served as a place where idols
were worshiped. Mount Sinai is
a low mountain, it never served
as a place of idol worship,
therefore it is the chosen
place.

A MIDRASH (Targum/Tosefta)

All of the mountains expected
to be chosen to be the place
where the Torah was given.
Mount Tavor said: "I am so tall
that the flood didn't even
cover half of me. I am the
right place. Mount Hermon
said: "I am the right choice,
God used me to divide the Yam
Suf. Mount Carmel said: "My
location is perfect, right for
either land or sea." Mount
Sinai didn't say anything. God
chose Mount Sinai because of
its humility. This made it the
right place.

**A. These midrashim add to the Torah without being based on
specific verses. What question are they trying to answer?**

_____

_____

**B. The rabbis wrote two different midrashim for the same
question. How could they believe that both were true?**

_____

_____

C. What value does each of these midrashim teach?

_____

_____

MISHPATIM is a sidra full of rules. It begins with the laws of
Hebrew slaves, a slave who volunteers to remain a slave and the
Hebrew maiden who is sold into slavery.

Next we are given a list of capitol crimes, these include:
murder, attempted murder, kidnapping, striking parents and being
publically disrespectful to parents.

Following that we are given a set of rules of damages. Here we
meet four famous Jewish characters: the goring ox, the pit, the
tooth and the fire.

Moving along, we have rules of theft and fraud. Also included
are rules about witchcraft, treatment of animals, opressing the
stranger, lending money, first born, carrying false rumors, fair
courts, the sabbatical year and even the 3 pilgrimage festivals.

Together these rules form the basis for a basic Jewish society.

At the end the sidra, God warns the people about following the
pagan customs of the nations around them, and promises to send
an angel ahead of them to protect them.

Finally, B'nai Yisrael accept the law and Moshe goes up Mount
Sinai to receive the Tablets of the law.

This sidra describes B'nai Yisrael becoming the choosing people
- the people who chose to accept the Torah. As you read the
description of their acceptance, see if you can figure out what
made them worthy.

Moshe went and repeated to the people
all the ordinances
and all the people answered with one voice:
"All the things the Lord has commanded - we will do."

                                        Exodus 24.3

What made B'nai Yisrael the right people to receive God's law?

_____
_____
_____
_____

A MIDRASH (Song of Songs R. 1:24)

God asked B'nai Yisrael: "Even though you want to accept the Torah, who will guarentee that you will keep your commitment?" B'nai Yisrael answered: "Our forefathers will be our guarantors."
God answered: "You forefathers need their own guarantors. Each of them doubted me. Avraham doubted that he would have a son, Yitzchak accepted Esav, and Ya'akov doubted when Yosef disappeared."
B'nai Yisrael then said: "How about the prophets."
God answered: "Your prophets often spoke for me but sometimes they fled like Yonah."
At this point, the children still in the wombs of their mothers spoke to God. "We will be the guarantors that the Torah will be studied and observed."
God answered: "This I will accept,"

A MIDRASH (Pirke d' Rabbi Eliezer 41)

The people listened and unanimously answered: **"Na'aseh V'nishma – we will do and we will hearken."** They said, we will observe and fulfill all the mitzvot in the Torah, even though we have not yet heard them.

(CLUE: Notice that it says We will do before it says we will listen.

A.   Underline the parts of these midrashim which are based directly on the Bible.

B.   What 2 explanations are we given why B'nai Yisrael was given the Torah?

_____
_____

C.   What does the second Midrash teach us about the way the rabbis who wrote the midrash view the Bible (and history)?

_____
_____
_____

D.   What is the message taught by each of these midrashim?

_____
_____
_____
_____

TERUMAH begins the description of the Mishkan. The sidra opens
with God directing Moshe to tell B'nai Yisrael to bring gifts
for the Mishkan. The Mishkan was to be a "dwelling place" for
God within B'nai Yisrael's camp. It was a portable sanctuary.
God asked for 13 different kinds of materials: (1) gold, (2)
silver, (3) copper, (4) blue yarn, (5) purple yarn, (6) crimson
yarn, (7) fine linen, (8) goats' hair, (9) tanned ram skins,
(10) dolphin skins, (11) acacia wood, (12) oil and spices. and
(13) stones for the breast plate.

The Torah then describes three items which will be used in the
Mishkan. These are the **Aron** - the ark which will be used to hold
the Torah, the **Shulchan** - the table which holds the 12 loaves of
shew bread which were brought daily, and the **Menorah** - the
candlestick with seven branches which was lighted in the
sanctuary.

Next the Torah describes the Mishkan itself. It is a tent with
20 columns on each of the long sides, and 6 on the one closed
wall. The top and the open side were covered with curtains.
The Mishkan was divided into two rooms, the holy of holies where
the ark was stored, and the holy - which was the remaining
2/3rds of the tent. There was a complicated plan of connectors
and fasteners which allowed it to be constructed and taken
appart - just like an erector set.

In addition, the sidra describes a copper altar with horns which
was used for sacrifices.

They shall make the ark of acacia wood
Two and a half cubits long and a cubit and a half wide
and a cubit high
Overlay it with pure gold.

Ex. 25.10-11

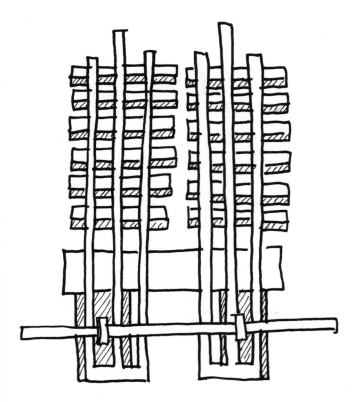

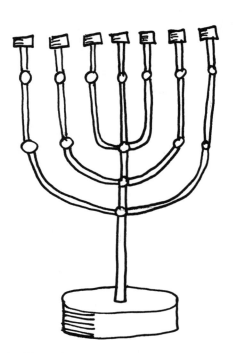

You shall make a lampstand of pure gold
the lampstand shall be made of hammered work
and its shat, its cups and petals
shall be one piece.

Ex. 25.31-32

You shall make a table of acacia wood
two cubits long and one cubit high
and a cubit and a half high.
Overlay it with pure gold
and make a gold molding for its rim.

Ex. 25.23-24

This week, the Torah describes the donations requested by God for the Mishkan. As you read the list, see (1) if you can believe that all of these things were findable in the wilderness, and (2) if you can figure out the reason for each item.

The Lord spoke to Moshe saying:
Tell the B'nai Yisrael to bring Me gifts
you shall accept gifts for Me from every person
        whose heart so moves him.
and these are the gifts that you shall accept form them: gold, silver, and copper; blue, purple, and crimson yarns, fine linen, goats' hair; tanned ram skins, dolphin skins, and acacia wood, oil for lighting, spices for the anointing oil and for the aromatic incense; lapis lazuli and other stones for setting the ephod and for the breastpiece.
And let them make Me a sanctuary
And I will dwell among them.
Exactly as I show you
the pattern of the Mishkan
and the pattern of all its furnishings
so you shall make it.
                    Exodus 25:1-9

   : Do you believe that it was really possible for B'nai Yisrael to donate all of these things in the wilderness? (Clue: Ex. 11.1-3).

_____

_____

2. What was the reason for asking for free will donations (and not demanding a fixed donation?

_____

_____

_____

A MIDRASH (Ex. R. 36.9)

When Moshe heard that a Mishkan was to be built in the midst of
the desert, he doubted that the community had enough materials
with which to build it. God told him: "Not only do B'nai
Yisrael collectively posses all the necessary materials to build
a Mishkan, but in fact - every single Jew is capable of
providing all that is needed to build a Mishkan."

A MIDRASH (Midrash Ha Gadol 25.1)

God asked for donations of 13 different kinds of materials
because each type of material was selected to help Israel atone
for a specific sin. This makes sense, because among other
things, the Mishkan was a place for making atonement.

     Gold = the golden calf
     Silver = the sale of Yosef for 22 pieces of silver
     copper = impurities in their hearts

(NOTE: This midrash then goes through the remainder of the 13
items).

A.   Underline the material which is based directly on the Torah.

**B.   According to these midrashim, how was it possible to build
the Mishkan in the wilderness.**

_____

_____

_____

**C. According to these midrashim, why did God ask for freewill
offering?**

_____

_____

_____

D.   What values are taught by these two midrashim?

_____

_____

_____

_____

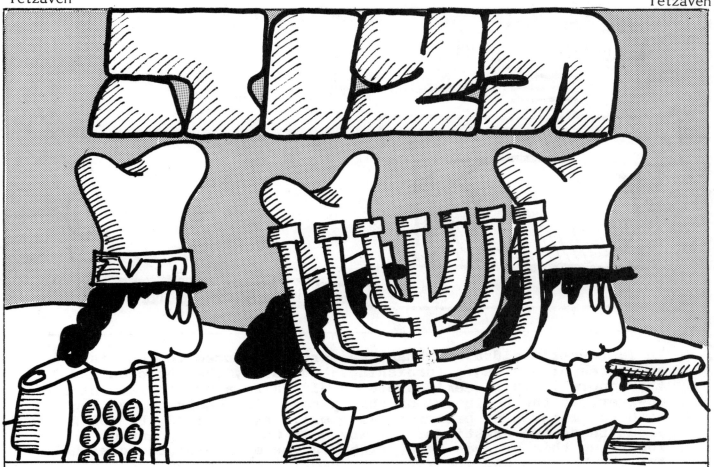

TETZAVEH is the second parasha which involves preparing the Mishkan. This time most of our focus is on the kohanim. First we have a special responsibility for B'nai Yisrael to bring olive oil for the **menora**.

Then Aharon, and his sons Nadav, Avihu, Eleazer and Itamar are chosen to serve as priests - Kohanim. Next we begin a long description of the special clothing a kohain was to wear. It included: the tunic, the breeches (the world's earliest description of underwear), the belt, the hat, the mantle (overgarment), the apron, the breast plate, and the head plate.

Following this there is a long description of the sacrifices and ceremonies which were used to consecrate the the Kohanim. At the end of the sidra we are introduced to the **mizbach hak'toret** - an altar for buring incense.

In last week's sidra, TERUMAH, we were introduced to the Mishkan
and three of its major furnishings: The aron, the shulchan and
the menorah. This week's sidra mainly talks about the kohanim.
However, at the beginning of this parasha is a passage dealing
with the mitzvah of bringing olive oil. As you read it, think
about these two questions: (1) Why does God make a point of
inserting this mitzvah here, right in the middle of the designs
for the Mishkan and its workers? and (2) Why is the Torah so
specific about the kind of oil which is to be used?

You shall command B'nai Yisrael
to bring you clear oil of beaten olives for lighting
for a **ner tamid**.
Aharon and his sons shall set them up in the Tent of Meeting,
outside the curtain
which is over the Tablets
(to burn) from evening to morning before the Lord.
It shall be an eteranal law for B'nai Yisrael
throughout all their generations.

                                   Exodus 27.20-21

1. Why do you think the Torah adds this mitzvah about olive oil
after the plans for the Mishkan and before the designs for the
kohanim?

_____

_____

2. What is so special about 'pure/clear beaten olive oil'? Why
do you think the Torah is so specific about this kind of oil?

_____

_____

_____

You shall make the MITZNEFET
of fine linen.

You shall make TZEETZ of pure gold and
engrave on it: "Holy to the Lord'

חדש לי

You shall make a CHOSHEN worked
into a design...set in it mounted
stones, in four rows of stones

They shall make the EPHOD of
gold, of blue, purple and crimson
yarns

You shall make the ME'IL of pure blue.
On its hem make pomegranates with
blue, purple and crimson yarns with bells
of gold between them

A MIDRASH (Midrash Hagadol 27.2)

God said to Moshe: "Let B'nai Yisrael eternally occupy
themselves with the mitzvah of bringing the olive oil. Through
it they will gain merit, and remember that the Mishkan is for
them and not just for the kohanim."

A MIDRASH (Ex. R. 36.1)

What kind of olive oil was usable in the Mishkan? Only the oil
which came from the first pressing of an olive could be used.
These first few drops were clear and had no sediment. So, when
you beat the olives, you got the clear oil. After this, the
olives needed to be ground and then filtered.

Why did God choose this oil for lighting?
The prophet Yermiyahu taught (11.15) that Yisrael is like an
olive. He said: "A fresh olive, a fruit of beautiful shape, did
God call your name."

How is Yisrael like olive oil?
Just like olive oil is the finest of all oils, so Israel is the
    holiest of all nations.
Most liquids when you mix them, mix together, but like oil
    Yisrael will never be absorbed into the other nations.
When you put liquids together, oil rises to the top, so too,
    Yisrael rises when they follow the Torah.
Just as oil serves to give light, Yisrael is a light to the
    nations.

**A. Underline the parts of these midrashim which are based on
facts or statements in the Bible.**

**B. How do these midrashim explain why this mitzvah is taught
here?**

_____

_____

**C. The second midrash uses a number of comparisons to show that
olive oil is used because it is like Yisrael. What do these
comparisons teach about Yisrael?**

_____

_____

_____

_____

_____

In KI TISSA we have new rules, more parts of the Mishkan and we even return to the on-going story of B'nai Yisrael in the wilderness. The sidra opens with rules for taking census. Moshe is told to collect a coin for each person rather than count the numbers directly.

Then we are introduced to a new Mishkan part - the **kiyor** - a laver for washing, and we are given the formula for making incense and the formula for making annointing oil.

Next we meet Betzalel, the skilled craftsman who headed the actual construction of the Mishkan. Next the focus changes and God restates the rules for observing Shabbat.

Now, the scene changes. We find Moshe still up on Mount Sinai (the end of the 40 days and 40 nights). God gives him the two tablets of the law. He takes them, heads down the mountain and finds the golden calf. Aaron had made the calf because the people were restless while Moshe was away. Moshe took the tablets and smashed the calf with them. They were destroyed.

Moshe then grinds up the calf, mixes it with water and makes the people drink. He then crticises Aharon and all the people. God then complains to the people. Moshe takes his tent and moves it away from everyone else. Moshe and God talk about B'nai Yisrael and what to do with them and then Moshe is sent back up the mountain to get a second set of commandments.

CONTINUED

At the end of the portion, we get a restatement of the covenant, a restatment of some key rules and a look at Moshe working on the new commandments on Mount Sinai.

NOW A TRUTH CAN BE TOLD. When you read the Torah, it seems that God gave Moshe the 10 commandments on Mount Sinai. When you hear people talk (and that talking is usually based on midrashim) you hear them speak about God giving the Torah to Moshe on Mount Sinai. Did God give just the 10 commandments or the whole Torah on Mount Sinai? When you read the midrashim (and the Torah text) closely, you can figure out that during the 40 days and 40 nights God taught the Torah to Moshe on Mount Sinai and gave him the 10 commandments to take back to B'nai Yisrael. As you read this text, here is the question for you to think about: Why did God only give 10 of the mitzvot in written form (at this point in time)?

When he finished speaking with him on Mount Sinai
God gave Moshe the two tablets of the covenant
stone tablets written with the finger of God.
                              Exodus 31:18

If God spent 40 days and 40 nights teaching Moshe on Mount Sinai, why was he only given 10 commandments to bring back to B'nai Yisrael.

_____

_____

_____

Why did God only give B'nai Yisrael the 10 commandments at Mount
Sinai and not the whole Torah?

To what can this be compared? This can be compared to a child
who just begins to go to school. At first, the teacher only
show him the letters of the alphabet on the blackboard. Later
when he has mastered these, the teacher gives him books. God
gave B'nai Yisrael the 10 commandments first, to teach them the
basic Torah-concepts, later God gave them the entire 5 books of
the Torah.

**A. This midrash works by comparison. Write down what is being
compared to what?**

_____
_____
_____
_____
_____

**B. Here are two questions to use to figure out what this
midrash teaches about the 10 commandments:**
        How important are the 10 commandments?

            _____
            _____

        Is it enough just to know the 10 commandments?

            _____
            _____

C. What is the message of this midrash?

    _____
    _____

In VAYAKHEL Moshe gathers B'nai Yisrael in order to teach two
things. First he teaches the rules for shabbat (again), then
he teaches the rules for donating to the Mishkan (again).
Following a review of these rules for donation, the Torah tells
us that the people indeed did give, and then it describes in
detail the actual work done by Betzalel and company. At one
point, Moshe has to tell B'nai Yisrael that there were too many
donations and no more would be accepted.

Among the interesting details - the **kiyor** - the laver was made
out of the copper taken from mirrors donated by the women.

What follows is the description of the actual work done on the tabernacle. As you read it, see if you can figure out (1) what it actually looked like, and (2) why the Torah teaches us all this detail about a place of worship which was used only in ancient times.

Then all the skilled among those engaged in the work made the Mishkan of ten strips of cloth, which they made of fine twisted linen, blue, purple, and crimson yarns; into these they worked a design of cherubim. The length of each cloth was four cubits, all cloths have the same measurements. They joined five of the cloths to one another, and they joined the other five cloths to one another. They made loops of blue wool on the edge of the outermost cloth of the one set, and did the same on the edge of the outermost cloth of the other set: they made fifty loops on the one cloth, and they made fifty loops on the edge of the end cloth of the other set, the loops being opposite one another. And they made fifty gold clasps and coupled the units to one another with the clasps, so that the Mishkan became whole. They made cloths of goats' hair for a tent ove the Mishkan; they made the cloths eleven in number. The length of each cloth was thirty cubits, and the width of each cloth was four cubits, the eleven cloths having the same measurements. They joined five of the cloths by themselves, and the other six cloths by themselves. They made fifty loops of the edge of the one set, and they made fifty loops on the edge of the end cloth of the other set. They made fifty copper clasps to couple the tent together so that it might become one whole. And they made a covering of tanned ram skins for the tent, and a covering of dolphin skins above.

They made the planks for the Mishkan of acacia wood, upright. The length of each plank was ten cubits, the width of each plank a cubit and a half. Each plank had two tenons, parallel to each other; they did the same with all the planks of the Mishkan. Of the planks of the Mishkan, they made twenty planks for the south side, making forty silver sockets under the twenty planks, two sockets under one plank for its two tenons and two sockets under each following plank for its two tenons; and for the other side wall of the Mishkan, the north side, twenty planks, with their forty silver sockets, two sockets under one plank and two sockets under each following plank, And for the rear of the Mishkan, to the west, they made six planks; and they made two planks for the corner of the Mishkan at the rear. They matched at the bottom, but terminated as one at the top into one ring; they did so with both of them at the two corners. Thus there were eight planks with their sockets of solver: sixteen sockets, two under each plank.

They made bars of acacia wood, five for the planks of the one side wall of the Mishkan, five bars for the planks of the other side wall of the Mishkan, and five bars for the planks of the wall of the Mishkan at the rear; to the west; they made the center bar to run, halfway up the planks, from end to end. They overlaid the planks with gold, and made their rings of gold, as holders for the bars; and they overlaid the bars with gold. They made the curtain of blue, purple, and crimson yarns, and fine twisted linen, working into it a design of cherubim. They made for it four posts of acacia wood and overlaid them with gold, with their hooks of gold; and they cast for them four silver sockets.

They made the screen for the entrance of the Tent, of blue, purple and crimson yarns, and fine twisted linen, done in embroidery; and five posts for it with their hooks. They overlaid their tops and their bands with gold; but the five sockets were of copper.

Exodus 38:8-38

BASED ON THIS TEXT, DRAW BLUEPRINTS FOR THE MISHKAN.

Why do you think the Torah goes into this much detail about the Mishkan?

_____

_____

A MIDRASH (Rav Bechi 38.9)

Although the mitzvot of the Mishkan are not ones that we can practice today, God gives us a reward for learning them. We are rewarded for studying the layout of the Mishkan and the design of furnishings and especially for studying their symbolic meaning.

The rabbis taught that someone who studies the laws of the sacrifices is considered to be equal to one who actually offered sacrifices. That means, that by studying about how people thanked God and made atonement through the Mishkan, we learn how to thank God and make atonement.

A. This midrash is really a comment on a problem. It tries to answer a question.

B. According to this midrash, why are all the details about the Mishkan important?

_____

_____

C. Do you agree with this midrash?

_____

_____

_____

D. What values does this midrash teach? (Even if you like the answer - do you like the values).

_____

_____

_____

PIKUDEI brings us to the end of the construction of the Mishkan, and the end of the book of Exodus. It begins with Moshe reporting to B'nai Yisrael how all the donations which were given were actually utilized in the Mishkan.

Then Moshe sets up the Mishkan and Aharon and his sons were established as the kohanim. At the end of the work, a cloud covered the Mishkan.

The sidra ends with a report that a cloud always covered the Mishkan by day and a fire would appear in it at night. This symbolized God's presence. Mishkan means dwelling place, and this showed that God dwelled with in the camp of B'nai Yisrael.

CHAZAK CHAZAK V'NITCHAZEK

At the end of the sidra, the Mishkan is erected and God's presence comes to rest on it. As you read the Torah's description of this moment, see if you can figure out what makes this moment so special.

When Moshe had finished the work
the cloud covered the Tent of Meeting
and the Presence of the Lord filled the Mishkan
And Moshe could not enter the Tent of Meeting
because the cloud had settled upon it
and the Presence of the Lord filled the Mishkan
When the cloud lifted from the Mishkan
B'nai Yisrael would set out on their various journeys;
but if the cloud did not lift
they would not set out until the day when it did lift
For over the Mishkan was a cloud of the Lord by day
and fire would appear in it by night
in the view of Bet Yisrael
throughout their journeys.

                    Exodus 40:33-38

Why do you think this the first time that God's presence is in the midst of B'nai Yisrael?

_____

_____

_____

A MIDRASH (Pesikta d'Rav Kahana 1.2)

(CLUE: SHECHINA = the presence of God which dwells among people)

God created the world so that His **shechina** could dwell there.
However, when Adam sinned, the **shechina** moved to the first
heaven. When the generation of Enosh sinned, the **shechina** moved
to the second heaven. When the generation of the flood was
wicked, the **shechina** moved to the third heaven. The evil of
the tower of Bavel moved the **shechina** to the fourth heaven.
When Egypt was corrupt in Avraham's time, the **shechina** moved to
the fifth heaven. The sins of Sodom moved the **shechina** to the
sixth heaven. And the wickedness of the Egyptians in the
generation of Moshe moved the **shechina** to the seventh heaven.

Avraham's goodness brought the **shechina** back to the sixth
heaven. Yitzchak's faithfulness brought the **shechina** back to
the fifth heaven. Ya'akov's returned the **shechina** to the
fourth heaven. Levi, who was founder of Moshe's tribe, brought
the **shechina** back to the third heaven. Kahat, Moshe's
grandfather, brought the **shechina** back to the second heaven.
Amram, Moshe's father, brought the **shechina** back to the first
heaven. When Moshe set up the Mishkan, the **shechina** again
returned to dwell on earth.

**A. Underline the parts of this midrash which are taken directly
from the Torah.**

**B. According to this midrash, why is this the right moment for
the shechina to appear?**

_____

_____

_____

**C. What does this midrash teach about the relationship between
God and people?**

_____

_____

_____

**D. What does this midrash teach about the importance of family
tradition?**

_____

_____

_____

ON ANOTHER PAGE, DESIGN A VIDEO GAME CALLED 7 HEAVENS

VAYIKRA starts the third book of the Torah. VAYIKRA is also a Torah portion which talks about sacrifices. Now that the Mishkan is completed, and now that the kohanim are in service - we are ready for description of their tasks.

In VAYIKRA we are introduced to 5 kinds of sacrifices:

The **Olah** - The burnt offering. This is the regular daily offering which is given as a freewill offering. This can be an ox, a lamb, a goat, a turtledove, or a pigeon.

The **Mincha** - The meal offering. This is an offering of flour and oil which is given by someone who cannot afford to give an animal.

The **Shlamim** - The peace offering. This is an offering which is given (like the **Olah**) except that it is devoted to peace. In midrash Tanchuma it says: "It is used by 2 friends who want to share a meal."

The **Chatat** - The sin offering. This is the offering of a person who broke a commandment - by doing something that was forbidden.

The **Asham** - The guilt offering. This is an offering of forgiveness for someone who stole, lied, opressed his neighbors or otherwise dealt falsely.

Here is the beginning of the Torah's description of the laws of sacrifice. As you read it, see if you can figure out which animals were chosen for sacrificing and why?

And the Lord called to Moshe
and spoke to him from the Tent of Meeting, saying:
"Speak to B'nai Yisrael and say to them:
When any of you presents an offering of cattle to the Lord
he shall choose his offering from the herd or from the flock.
If his offering is a burnt offering from the herd,
he shall make his offering an ox without blemish.
He shall bring it to the entrance of the Tent of Meeting,
that it will be accepted before the Lord
If his offering for a burnt offering is from the flock
of sheep or of goats
he shall make his offering a male without blemish.
                                    Leviticus 1:1-3&10

1. List the three kinds of animals which were used for sacrifice? (In biblical terms birds are not animals - they are birds).
_____

_____

2. Why do you think these three animals were chosen?
_____

_____

A MIDRASH (Pesikta d'Rav Kahana)

God said: "There are 10 kinds of kosher animals, but only three
of them are domesticated. Because I don't want you hunting the
wild beasts of the hills and fields, I will take only the ox,
the sheep and the goat as my sacrifices.

A MIDRASH (Sifre 54)

Each of these three animals teach us something about our
forefathers. The ox reminds us of Avraham's welcoming guests,
because he ran and got an ox to serve his 3 guests. The lamb
reminds us of Yitzchak who had a ram sacrificed instead of him.
And the goat reminds us of Ya'akov who serves his father two kid
goats when he received the blessing.

**A.   Underline the parts of these midrashim which are taken
directly from the Torah.**

**B.   According to these midrashim, why were these three animals
chosen.**

_____
_____
_____
_____

C.   What messages are taught by these midrashim:

_____
_____
_____
_____
_____

In TZAV we are introduced to what the kohanim have to do in the
Mishkan. We are introduced to the ritual of the **olah** sacrifice.
Here, the offering is left burning all through the night, and in
the morning the kohain must remove the ashes. The kohain must
keep the fire burning constantly, and the fat parts of the **olah**
are turned into the smoke of the **shlamim**.

Then the rules for the **mincha** offering are given. The kohanim
make cakes out of flour and oil and put it on the altar with
frankincense. That which is left over they may eat. As part of
the rules of the **mincha** offering we learn about the special
offering which is made when a kohain is anointed.

Next comes the rules of the **chatat** offering. This offering is
slaughtered, sacrificed and eaten by the kohanim. The rules for
the **asham** offering are similar except that key parts of the
animal are burnt totally into smoke. Finally we get the rules
for the **shlamim** sacrifice. This includes the commandment to eat
that which is sacrificed on the day it was offered (or in the
case of a freewill offering within two days).

As long as we have been talking about sacrificing animals, the
Torah introduces some rules of how to eat meat. No meat may be
eaten from an animal which died naturally or which was torn by
wild animals. Also, no blood may ever be consumed.

TZAV ends with the inauguration of Aharon, the kohanim, and
Mishkan.

To understand something about this text, you will have to go back and look at parshat VAYIKRA. Notice to whom all the commands are directed. Who is left out? As you read this text, see if you can find a new emphasis.

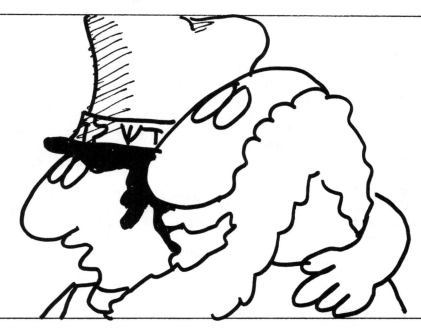

And the Lord spoke to Moshe saying:
"Command Aharon and his sons saying:
'This is the ritual of the burnt offering:
The burnt offering itself shall remain where it is burned upon the altar all night until morning,
while the fire on the altar is kept going on it.
The kohain shall dress in linen raiment,
with linen breeches next to his body;
and he shall take up the ashes to which the fire has reduced the burnt offering on the altar and place them beside the altar.
He shall then take off his garments and put on other garments,
and carry the ashes outside the camp to a clean place.
The fire on the altar shall be kept burning, not to go out:
every morning the priest shall feed wood to it,
And lay out the burnt offering on it,
and turn into smoke the fat parts of the offerings of the peace-offerings.
A perpetual fire shall be kept burning on the altar,
it shall not go out
                              Leviticus 6:1-6

Who was left out of sidrat Vayikra and added here?

_____

_____

Why do you think that "he" was left out and then added?

_____

_____

_____

A MIDRASH (Tosafot Ha Rosh)

When God was teaching Moshe the laws which were taught in
VAYIKRA, Moshe asked: "What type of wood is suitable for a
sacrifice?" God informed him: "All kinds except for the wood of
grape vines and olive branches. Those two may not be burned on
the altar. They are special because of the fruits which they
produce. Branches of the grape vine may not be used since they
supply wine for the nesachim (libations); neither may olive
wood, for the olive yields oil for the menora and the mincha
offerings."
Moshe immediately argued, "Master of the Universe, it seems that
your words should apply to people as well. You honored the
grape vine and olive tree because of their produce. Should You
then not treat Aharon in an honorable way (and address him
directly) in spite of Your anger at him if only for the sake of
his worthy sons?"
God accepted this argument and addressed Aharon in TZAV.

**A.   Underline the parts of this midrash which are taken from the
Torah.**

B.   What question is this midrash trying to answer?
_____
_____

C.   What answer does it give?
_____
_____

D.   What does this midrash teach about Moshe?
_____
_____

**E.   What does this midrash teach about God's relationship with
Moshe?   (Does it remind you of Avraham?)**
_____
_____
_____

F.   What is the "moral" of this midrash?
_____
_____

In SHMINI we see the final day of decication of the Mishkan.
There are all kinds of sacrifices and ceremonies. Following
these festivities, two of Aharon's sons, Nadav and Avihu enter
the Mishkan on their own, and offer a "strange fire" before the
Lord. They are burnt to death. God then warns Aharon that no
kohain should drink before doing priestly service. Then Moshe
orders the kohanim back to work.

Then the Lord teaches Aharon and Moshe a long list of rules
about what animals can be eaten. First we are given the list of
permitted animals - the basic rule being that the animal must
chew its cud and have a cleft hoof. Then we are told about
fish. To be eaten, a fish must have both fins and scales. Next
we are given rules about birds - we are given a list of birds
which cannot be eaten. All of the forbidden birds are hunters.
Continuing its evaluation of permissible animals, the Torah
lists the kinds of insects which can be eaten. It also forbids
all reptiles and a bunch of animals which are in the rat and
mole category.

Finally the Torah talks about things which become unclean
through contact with the carcass of an unclean animal.

In this sidra, two of Aharon's sons are killed in an accident in the Mishkan. Immediately after this, God gives a set of rules to Aharon. Then Moshe gave him a set of orders. As you read the text, see if you can figure out why Moshe gave these orders rather than words of comfort.

And the Lord spoke to Aharon, saying:
"Drink no wine or other alcoholic beverage,
you or your sons with you,
when you enter the Tent of Meeting,
so that you don't die
it is a law for all time throughout your generations
For you must make a distinction between the holy and the ordinary
and between the unclean and the clean
and you must teach B'nai Yisrael all the laws which the Lord has taught them through Moshe.

And Moshe spoke to Aharon
and to his remaining sons, Eleazar and Itamar:
Take the meal offering that is left over from the Lord's offerings by fire
and eat it unleavened beside the altar
for it is most holy.
And you shall eat it in the holy place
because it is your due
and that of your children

Leviticus 10:8-1

Why do you think Moshe chose this moment to give these orders to Aharon and his remaining sons?

_____

_____

_____

A MIDRASH

Why did Moshe give orders to Aharon and his sons, that they
should again perform the sacrfices?

To what can this be compared? This can be compared to a husband
and wife who had a fight. The husband told the wife: Leave the
house at once,"   After some time, the husband's anger abated
and she returned to the house. When she returned, she again did
the cooking and cleaning and was happy. When Aharon and his
sons could return to their Divine service, they were again
happy.

**A. This midrash is another comparison. Explain who or what
each of the followingrepresents:**
    Aharon =

    God =

    The Sacrifices =

B.   What is the message of this midrash?

_____

_____

Welcome to TAZRIA, the first of two sidrot on leprosy and
related topics. In this sidra we have a lot of laws regarding
purity. They include:

A woman is impure for 7 days following the birth of a son, who
is then circumcised on the eighth day. She is impure for 2
weeks following the birth of a daughter. To become pure, she
has the kohain offer proper sacrifices.

Then the Torah introduces rules of skin disease. We get a list
of various kinds of conditions which can be considered leprosy.
This is the procedure. The person with the problem comes to the
kohain who decides if the problem is indeed leprosy. If the
kohain has concerns, the person is isolated and re-examined in 7
days. If the conditions has ended, the kohain calls him clean,
but if the rash has spread, the kohain labels him a leper.

The person who has leprosy tears his clothes, shaves his head,
covers his lip and must call out "Unclean, Unclean" wherever he
goes. He has to dwell outside the camp.

The kohain is responsible to see to it that the leper and all
that comes in contact with him is separated from the rest of the
community.

In TAZRIA we talk about skin disease and label some of it
leprosy. This is the way the Torah introduces the topic, read
it carefully and then compare it to the passage which follows

And the Lord spoke to Moshe and Aharon saying:
When a person has on the skin of his body
a swelling, a rash, or a discoloration -
and it develops into a scaly infection on the skin of his body
it shall be reported to Aharon the kohain
or to one of his sons - the kohanim
The priest shall examine the infection on the skin of his body
if the hair in the affected area has turned white
and the infection appears to be deeper than the skin of his body
it is leprosy.
                    Lev. 13.1-3

Now read what this text from Eccl. 5.5, and see what it says
about skin-disease.

It is better not to make a vow at all
than to vow and not fulfill.
Do not let your mouth cause your flesh to feel guilt
And don't tell the messenger that it was an error
Fear God and don't let God be angered by your talk
and destroy your possessions.

In Tazrea and in the next sidra Metzora, the Torah talks about
leprosy of the skin, of houses, and of clothing. Based on this
text from Kohelet can you see a connection between peoples words
and these kinds of leprosy?

_____
_____
_____
_____

A MIDRASH (Lev. R. 17.3)

There are 10 sins which can cause leprosy:

1. Serving Idols (with words). Those who worshiped the golden calf got leprosy (from Ex. 32.25)

2. Lack of modesty. The daughters of Yerushalaim got leprosy for behaving poorly (from Is. 3.17)

3. Bloodshed. Yoav got leprosy for murder (II Sam. 3.29)

4. Profaning God's name. This happened to Gehazi who was Elisha's servant. (from II Kings 5.27)

5. Cursing God. This happened to the Philistines. (from 1 Sam. 7.46)

6. Robbing the Public. This happened to Shevna who stole from the Mishkan. (from Is. 22.17)

7. Stealing an honor. This happened to King Uzia (II Chron. 26.21)

8. Conceit. This too we learn from King Uzia (II Chron. 26.16)

9. Lashon Hara. This we learn from when Miriam slandered Moshe (Num. 12.1)

10. Being a Miser. This we learn from the description of house leprosy (in this sidra).

A. When the rabbis wrote this midrash, they found ten places in the bible where they believed that God used leprosy as a punishment for breaking important Torah-rules. Decide which of these are really described in the Torah, and which are based on other midrashim on the passages quoted. Circle those which are examples really found in the Torah.

B. By bringing in these 10 examples and by comparing TAZRIA to the quotation from Kohelet, what have the rabbis done to the meaning of this passage?

_____
_____
_____
_____

C. What is the message of this midrash?

_____

_____

_____

D. What important Jewish value can be learned by comparing the Kohelet text with this sidra?

_____

_____

_____

_____

In TAZRIA, the last sidra, we learned all about leprosy, in this parasha - METZORA, we learn how the kohanim are supposed to cure leprosy. First the kohain has to go and inspect the leprosy, to see if it is indeed passed. Then he performs a cleansing ritual; he has the patient wash, shave and clean his clothes. Then the patient waits in isolation for seven days. On day eight, the kohain performs a whole number of rituals including **mincha** and **asham** offerings.

Then the Lord teaches Moshe and Aharon all about house leprosy. This is when "green or red stuff" starts growing on the walls of a house. Just like in the case of people leprosy, the kohain comes in and inspects the situation. If it is leprosy, the kohain has the house sealed for 7 days. If it doesn't heal itself, their are a whole set of rules about isolating stones and replastering. When the matter is finished, the kohain has to go through other ritual actions.

The sidra ends with a list of discharges from the body which require acts of purification.

In this sidra, you will find one phrase repeated over and over again. As you read the Torah text, (1) find the phrase, (2) see how many times it is repeated, and (3) see what conclusions you can draw.

LEV. 13.59

This is the **Torah**/law of leprosy of cloth, wool or linen
in the warp or in the woof
or of any article of skin
for pronouncing it clean or unclean.

LEV. 14.2

This is the **Torah**/law of purifying a leper
at the time he is to be cleaned.
When it has been reported to the kohain
the kohain shall go outside the camp.
If the kohain sees that the leper has been healed of his scaly affliction
the kohain shall order two live clean birds

LEV. 14.32

This is the **Torah**/law of a poor person who has leprosy

LEV. 14.54

This is the **Torah**/law for every plague of leprosy
for a scall, and for leprosy of a garment
or a house
for swellings, for rashes or for discoloration
to determine if they are clean or unclean.

LEV. 14.57

This is the **Torah**/of leprosy.

1. What phrase is repeated?_____

2. How many times is it repeated?_____

3. Can you draw a conclusion from this?

_____
_____
_____

A MIDRASH (Lev. R. 16.6)

Rabbi Joshua ben Levi said: "The word Torah is used five times in regard to the plague of leprosy. We know that leprosy **metzora = motze-shem-ra** - one who spreads evil reports. The repetition of **Torah** five times in connection to leprosy is meant to teach that one who spreads evil reports is just like someone who broke all the laws in all five books of the Torah."

A. Underline those parts of this midrash which are based on "Torah-facts."

B. What does this midrash notice about this sidra?
_____
_____

C. What does Rabbi Joshua learn from this insight?
_____
_____
_____

D. What kind of rules does this midrash use for studying Torah?
_____
_____
_____

ACHRE MOT means after the death. After the death of Nadav and
Avihu God begins this sidra by giving Aharon additional roles
about the way the kohanim should perform their functions. These
include coming into the Mishkan only at the fixed times and
wearing the proper clothing.

Then we get a description of the responsibilities of the kohain
ha-gadol on Yom Kippur. These include his own purification, and
the choosing of the two goats: the one to become the **chatat**
offering, and the one to become the 'scape-goat.' Following a
detailed description of all the priestly functions, we are also
told how B'nai Yisrael is to fast and make atonement.

Following a discussion of these sacrifices, we get a couple of
laws about blood. You are required to cover the blood of an
animal you slaughter, and it is forbidden to consume any blood.
(It is interesting that laws of sacrifice are almost always
followed by laws of eating meat).

Next we get a set of prohibitions called the nakednesses. These
all have to do with sexual conduct. The parasha ends with a
description of Eretz Yisrael, and how this land will not
tolerate wrong doing.

This sidra includes a set of things which Jews are not supposed to do - called the nakednesses. If you want to know what they are - look them up in Leviticus 18. In that passage, God is really concerned that B'nai Yisrael not follow some of the customs of the people who lived in Canaan before they took it and made it Eretz Yisrael. Following those rules, God gives this warning about the land. As you read this text, see if you can figure out what is being said about Eretz Yisrael.

Don't disgrace yourselves in any of those things
for it is by those things that the nations are defiled
those which I am casting out before you
This is how the land became defiled;
and I called it to account for its evilness,
and the land spit out its inhabitants.
Therefore you must keep My laws and My norms,
and you must not do any of those disgusting things,
neither the citizen nor the stranger who resides among you;
for all those disgusting things were done by the people who were
in the land before you and the land became defiled.

So let not the land spit you out for defiling it,
as it spit out the nation that came before you.

Lev. 18.24-28

In this passage, what is said about the land of Yisrael?

_____

_____

A MIDRASH (Midrash Agada 18:4/Shabbat 33b)

Of all the lands in the world, Eretz Yisrael is the most holy.
She is therefore sensitive to any evil committed on her soil.
If her inhabitants become evil and do wrong, she is unable to
"stomach" them. She therefore inevitably "spits them up," and
the are exiled. (This happens twice to B'nai Yisrael).

A MIDRASH (Shabbat 36b)

Eretz Yisrael is the Palace of the King. A sin which may be
tolerated elsewhere calls for immediate punishment in the Land
of Holiness.

A. Underline the "Torah" parts of these midrashim.

B. One of these midrashim uses comparisons. Explain the
comparisons:

_____
_____
_____
_____

C. What do these midrashim teach about Eretz Yisrael?
_____
_____

D. What Jewish value do these midrashim teach?
_____
_____

KEDOSHIM is the sidra which is known as the holiness code. It
begins with Moshe gathering all of B'nai Yisrael together and
teaching them laws which will make them holy. These laws are
held together by a chorus line: "I am the Lord"

These laws include: respecting parents, not worshiping idols,
observing Shabbat, eating sacrifices right away, leaving the
corners of your field, not stealing, not taking advantage of
handicaps, judging cases fairly, not hating people, loving your
neighbor as your self.

Then we move into other laws such as: mixed breeding, treatment
of slaves, forbidding the fruit of new trees, not eating blood,
not doing witchcraft, not shaving the corners of your head,
respecting your daughter, not turning to ghosts, rising before
the aged, being fair to the stranger, and using fair weights and
measures.

We are to follow all these laws, because (1) God took us out of
Egypt, and (2) they will make us holy like God.

At the end of the sidra we get a few more laws. We cannot
follow the cult of Molech - a cult where parents sacrificed
their first born children, we are not to embarass our parents,
and we have a larger list of unacceptable sexual relationships.

At the very end, God explains that all these laws were given to us because (1) we are going into a land of milk and honey, (2) they make us different than other nations, and (3) they make us holy.

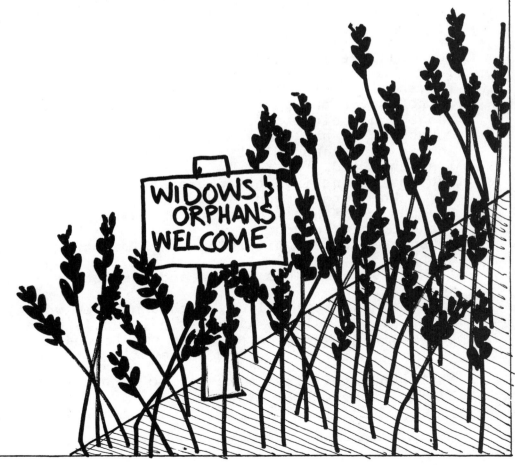

This passage is called the holiness code. Most laws that were taught to B'nai Yisrael were taught to anyone who would listen to Moshe when he was teaching. As you read this text, see if you can figure out why God thought this passage was important enough for all Jews to hear, and therefore told Moshe to speak to the whole community of B'nai Yisrael.

The Lord spoke to Moshe, saying:
Speak to the whole community of B'nai Yisrael and say to them:
You shall be holy, for I, the Lord you God, am holy.
Each of you shall fear his/her mother and father and all of you
shall keep my Shabbatot
I the Lord am your God.
Do not turn to idols
or make molten gods for yourselves:
I the Lord am your God.
When you reap the harvest of your land,
you shall not reap all the way to the edges of your field,
or gather the gleanings of your harvest.
You shall not pick your vineyard bare,
or gather the fallen fruit of your vineyard,
you shall leave them for the poor and the stranger:
I the Lord am your God.
You shall not steal;
you shall not deal falsely or lie to one another.
You shall not swear falsely by My name,
profaning the name of your God:
I am the Lord.
You shall not oppress your neighbor nor rob him
The wages of a laborer shall not remain with you until morning.
You shall not insult the deaf,
or place a stumbling block before the blind.
You shall fear your God:
I am the Lord.
You shall not render an unfair decision in courts:
do not favor the poor or show deference to the rich;
judge your neighbor fairly.
Do not go up and down as a talebearer among your people
And do not stand idly by the blood of your neighbor:
I am the Lord.
You shall sanctify yourselves and be holy,
for I the Lord am your God.
You shall faithfully observe My laws:
I the Lord make you holy.
If any man curses his father or his mother, he shall be put to
death;
if he has cursed his father and his mother - his bloodguilt is
upon him.
If a man commits adultery with a married woman,
committing adultery with his neighbor's wife,
the man and the woman shall be put to death.

Leviticus 19:1-4 & 9-15 & 20:7-10

What about this text makes it so important that all of B'nai Yisrael had to hear it?

_____

_____

A MIDRASH: (Torah Timima)

God told Moshe: "For this sidra do not follow your traditional teaching methods. Instead call an assembly of the entire people including the women and children. This parasha is important for two reasons: (1) It teaches the concept: "Love your neighbor as youself" and (2) It teaches all the same rules as the 10 commandments.

This midrash presents a puzzle, see if you can find all of the 10 commandments in this passage. Copy the passage from KEDOSHIM next the commandment it matches. (If you need help, use the numbers to look them up)

1. I am the Lord (19.3) _____

2. No other Gods (19.4) _____

3. No God's name in vain (19.12) _____

4. Shabbat (19.3) _____

5. Honor Parents (19.3) _____

6. Don't Murder (19.16) _____

7. No Adultery (20.10) _____

8. Don't Steal (19.11) _____

9. No Falsewitness (19.16)_____

10. Don't Covet (19.18)_____

What did you learn from this sidra?

_____
_____
_____
_____
_____

With parshat EMOR we are back to talking about rules for
kohanim. God tells Aharon and sons that they may only be in the
presence of a dead person if it is a close relative, because
they must remain holy to offer sacrifices. Kohanim cannot marry
a harlot or a divorced woman. The kohain ha-gadol is given even
stricter rules.

Next the Torah lists a long group of physical defects which can
keep a person from the family of kohanim from working as a
priest. Then it is made clear which food can only be eaten by
the kohanim, and which can be eaten by all of B'nai Yisrael.

Having finished with rules of the kahuna (priesthood), the Torah
moves on to Jewish holidays. We get the basic rules for
Shabbat, Pesach, counting the omer, Shavuot, Yom Kippur and
Sukkot. This is followed by a restatement to leave food for
those in need.

Moving back to the Mishkan, we get another statement of the rule
to bring olive oil for light, and of the 12 loaves of the shew
bread.

To end the sidra, we have the story of a Ben Yisrael who takes
God's name in vain and who is stoned by the community.

**In this sidra we are taught the laws for many of the Jewish
holidays. Read this text and see of you can figure out the rule
which is being taught.**

You shall keep count
from the day after the Shabbat,
from the day that you bring the sheaf of wave offering,
for seven full weeks
you shall count fifty days,
until the day after the seventh week;
then you shall bring an offering of new grain to the Lord.
                              Leviticus 23:15-16

Write the rule here:

_____
_____
_____
_____
_____
_____
_____

HERE ARE A COUPLE OF CLUES:

1. The day after Shabbat - the day of waving = the 2nd day of
Pesach.

2. The day after 7 weeks = Shavuot

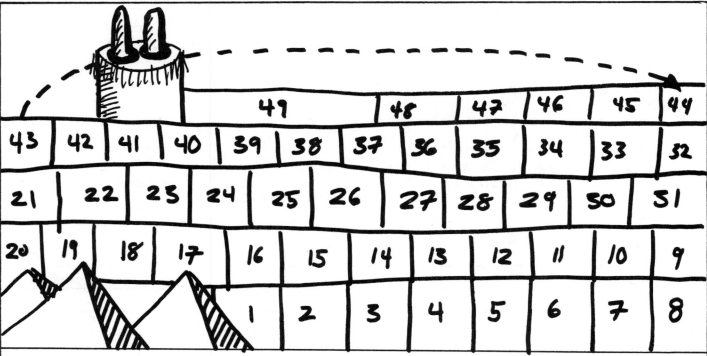

A MIDRASH (Sefer Ha Hinuch ad loc)

It is a mitzva to count forty-nine days starting from the day of
the offering of the omer, the sixteenth of Nissan, which is the
second day of Pesach. The mitzva is to count both the number
of days and the number of weeks.

What is the reason for the counting?
When B'nai Yisrael were redeemed from Egypt, Moshe told them
that they were to be given the Torah after forty-nine days.
They began counting on the day after the first seder, Pesach:
and finished their counting on Shavuot - the day the Torah was
given. In their great anticipation to receive that Divine gift,
each Jew kept a daily count for himself, waiting for the great
4ay to arrive. Thereafter, the counting was instituted by God
as a permanent mitzva.

A. Underline the parts of this midrash which <u>cannot</u> be found in
the Torah or which cannot be supported directly from the Torah.

B. What did this midrash teach you about some laws in the
Torah?

_____
_____
_____

C. What "message" can be learned from this law (with help from
the midrash)?

_____
_____
_____
_____

BEHAR is a short sidra which gives us a few new rules. We are
introduced to the sabbatical year. Every seventh year the land
is allowed to rest and no farming is done. Then we meet the
jubilee year. The jubilee year is the 50th year (the year after
the seventh sabbatical year). It is a year where not only is
there no farming, but where all slaves go free and all debts are
canceled.

Next we are told about the rules of owning property in the land
of Israel. It can never be permanantly sold. It must always
return to the family to whom it originally was given. This is
true of houses, lands and even people.

Then, we get a strong statement about never lending money for
interest. The sidra ends with another warning not to worship
idols.

In this parasha, God gives a law about not lending money for interest. If you read it closely, you will notice that God connects this rule to the fact that God took B'nai Yisrael out of Egypt. As you read the text, see if you can figure out the connection.

If your brother,
falls into hard times
and you have financial control of him
you hold him like a stranger
so he acts as your slave
Do not take from him any interest,
but fear your God.
Let him stay under you as your brother.
Do not lend him money with interest,
or give him your food at interest.
I the Lord am you God who brought you out of the land of Egypt,
to give you the land of Canaan,
to be your God.

                                        Leviticus 25:35-38

1. What is the connection between being taken out of Egypt and not lending money at interest?

_____

_____

_____

2. What do you think is so bad about collecting interest?

_____

_____

A MIDRASH (Ex. R. 31:13)

The Hebrew word for interest is
 נֶשֶׁךְ neshech, it is very close
to the word נָשַׁךְ nashach, which
means bite. God warns Yisrael,
do not "bite" like the snake and
offer someone a loan with interest.
In the end, you will own his
house, his fields, and his vine-
yards because he cannot make the
interest payments.

A MIDRASH (Ex. R. 31:15)

If a Jew takes an interest on a
loan, and breaks this mitzvah,
that Jew denies that God took
us out of Egypt. In Egypt we
were forced to work and own
nothing, taking money on
interest turns people back into
slaves.

If a Jew breaks a mitzvah, God
calls together a heavenly court
to judge the actions. However,
if a Jew lends money for
interest, God quotes Yechezkel
(18:13) and says "He has given
money on interest...he shall
not live." No court is called.

**A. Underline the parts of these midrashim which are based on
the Torah.**

B. What is the connection between "Egypt" and "interest"?

_____
_____
_____

C. Why is the Torah so concerned about "interest"?

_____
_____
_____

D. How can you apply this concern today?

_____
_____
_____

BECHUKOTAI is the last sidra in Leviticus. It comes to an end
by giving a list of blessings which B'nai Yisrael will receive
if they follow God's laws, and a list of curses which will
happen if they don't follow the Torah.

We are promised five blessings: (1) the land giving lots of
food, (2) peace in the land, (3) victory or enemies, (4)
economic and population growth, and (5) God's presence among
them.

Then we are given a long list of more than 32 different curses.

The portions ends by talking about (1) vows which a person
takes, (2) vows a person makes about offering things to God, (3)
dedicating things to God, and things which are to be (4) tithed
or (5) redeemed. The kohanim were involved in all five of
these functions.

CHAZAK CHAZAK V'NITCHAZEK

In this sidra, God gives Israel a promise of blessings if they follow the laws of the Torah, and curses if they break the laws of the Torah. One of these promises is to give "rains in their season." As you read this text see if you can figure out what this means.

If you follow My laws and faithfully observe My commandments,
I will give you rains in their season,
and that the earth shall yield its produce
and the trees of the field shall yield their fruit.
Your harvesting grain shall last till the grapes are ripe
and your harvesting grapes shall last till it is time to plant grain
you shall eat your fill of bread
and dwell safely in your land.
I will give peace in the land,
and you shall lie down unafraid of anyone;
I will get rid of all the vicious beasts in the land
and no sword shall cross your land.
You shall chase to your enemies,
and they shall fall before you by the sword.
Five of you shall give chase to a hundred,
and a hundred of you shall give chase to ten thousand;
And your enemies shall fall before you by the sword.
I will look with favor upon you,
and make you fertile and multiply you;
and I will maintain My covenant with you.
You shall eat old grain long stored,
and you shall have to clear out the old to make room for the new.
I will establish My Mishkan among you
and I will not spurn you.
I will walk among you
And I will be your God,
and you shall be My people.

             Leviticus 26:3-12

How would you explain "Rain in their seasons."

_____
_____
_____
_____

A MISHNEH (Taanit 1.5)

On the third of the month of Cheshvan they may say the prayer
for rain. Rabban Gamaliel taught, One can pray for rain on the
seventh day of the month, this is fifteen days after the end of
Sukkot and this gives enough time so that all of B'nai Yisrael
who made a pilgrimage to Yerushalim can make it back to Babylon
and cross the River Euphrates. This is the right season for
rain.

Why would it be the wrong season for rain before the 15th?

_____

_____

_____

What concern does this mishnah teach?

_____

_____

_____

A MIDRASH (Ex. R. 35:10)

THEN I WILL GIVE YOUR RAINS IN THEIR SEASON means, during the
nights. In the days of King Herod the rains used to fall at
night. In the morning a wind blew, the clouds were scattered,
the sun shone, the earth dried up and the labourers went out and
engaged in their work, conscious that their labours were
agreeable to their Father in heaven.

What value does this midrash teach?

_____

_____

_____

**How does this midrash change the meaning of the word
z'man – which can be translated as either time or season?**

_____

_____

_____

BAMIDBAR is the first parasha in Numbers. It begins with Moshe
and Aharon taking a census of all the males over twenty.
According to the biblical census bureau: Reuven - 46,500,
Shimon - 59,300, Gad - 45,650, Yehudah - 74,600, Issachar -
54,400, Zevulun - 57,400, Efraim - 40,500, Manashe - 32,200,
Binyamin - 35,400, Dan - 62,700, Asher - 41,500, and Naphtali -
53,400.

(We interrupt this description for a short quiz:

    1.   What tribe is missing?_____

    2.   Why aren't they counted? _____

    3.   Yosef is not missing,

        why isn't he mentioned?_____

    4.   In total how many are there?_____)

Next we are given the locations of the various tribes around the
Mishkan when they are camped. (See the chart)

Then we review the family of Aharon and their responsibilities,
and meet a few other clans which are connected to the Kohanim.

To end the sidra, Moshe is ordered to take a seperate survey of
the kohanim and then the orders for breaking camp are given.

If you read this text carefully, you will notice something
funny. It introduces the children of Moshe and Aharon and then
lists only Aharon's sons. See if you can read this text and
then explain this problem.

These are the offspring of Aharon and Moshe
on the day that Lord spoke with Moshe on Mount Sinai.
These were the names of Aharon's sons:
Nadav the first born
and Avihu,
Eleazar and Itmar;
those were the names of Aharon's sons,
the anointed kohanim who were ordained for the priesthood.
But Nadav and Avihu died before the Lord
when they offered alien fire before the Lord
in the wilderness of Sinai;
and they left no children.
So it was Eleazar and Itmar who served as kohanim in the
presence of of their father Aharon.

                                        Numbers 3:1-4

Write your own midrashic explanation of this:

_____
_____
_____
_____
_____
_____
_____
_____
_____
_____
_____
_____

A MIDRASH (Sanhendrin 19b)

Even though the Torah lists only the sons of Aharon, they can be considered the children of both Moshe and Aharon. They are called the sons of Moshe because he taught them the Torah. This tells us that whoever teaches the Torah to the son of a fellow man Torah, is regarded as though he had been his father.

A. Find proof in the Torah that Moshe taught Torah to Aharon's sons.

_____
_____
_____

B.   What Jewish value is being taught here?

_____
_____
_____

N

BINYAMIN ASHER DAN NAFTALI ISJACHAR

MERARITES

EFRAIM GERSHOMITES SONS OF AHARON / AHARON & MOSHE YEHUDA

THE MISHKAN

KOHATHITES

MANASHE GAD RE'UVEN SHIMON ZEVULUN

New we have come to sidrat NASO which is a collection of
different kinds of material. Moshe is ordered to take a census
of the clans of Gersomites, Merates, and Kohatites. All of
these are from the tribe of Levi and had special duties for
moving parts of the Mishkan when B'nai Yisrael traveled.

Next we get an assortment of rules including: removing corpses
from camp, paying damages, the sota test for adultery, and the
vows of the nazir.

At this point the Torah introduces the **birkat kohanim**. Then we
get some special responsibilities of the chieftains, followed by
the special gifts each of them brought. (There is a day to day
description of their gifts in the text).

At the end of the sidra we are told that Moshe could talk to God
in the tent of meeting and hear God's voice coming from between
the two cherubim on the **aron**.

Read this text carefully. See if you can figure out who these new chieftans are and why they have special offerings.

And it came to pass
on the day that Moshe finished setting up the Mishkan,
and had anointed it and made it holy
and also all its furnishings,
as well as the altar and its utensils.
He had anointed them and made them holy
The chieftains of Yisrael,
the heads of ancestral houses,
namely, the chieftains of the tribes,
those who were in charge of the **numbers**,
They came forward
and brought their offering before the Lord:
                                        Numbers 7:1-3

Make your own best guess who these leaders who were in charge of numbers were. Why do you think they had a special privilege?
_____
_____
_____
_____

A MIDRASH (Bamidbar Rabbah 12,20, 15,16)

The chieftains of the tribes were those who were appointed over
B'nai Yisrael in Egypt. These were the men whom the Torah was
talking about when it says: "And the officers of B'nai Yisrael,
whom Pharaoh's taskmasters had set over them were beaten,
saying: Wherefore have you not fulfilled your appointed task in
making bricks both yesterday and today...?" (Exodus 5,14). They
had to stand and count the bricks which were produced each day.
When Pharaoh ordered B'nai Yisrael to make the same number of
bricks each day without using straw. The officers refused to
tell who had not produced enough bricks. For this, the
taskmasters would then beat them. These officers said: "It is
better for us to be beaten rather than for the rest of the
people should suffer."

A. How does this midrash use the word "number" to join two
different stories in the Torah?

_____
_____
_____

B. According to this midrash, why were the chieftains honored?

_____
_____
_____

C. What kind of role models are these chieftans? What value
does the midrash teach us through their example?

_____
_____
_____